ORIGINS OF THE AMERICAN INDIANS

European Concepts, 1492–1729

LATIN AMERICAN MONOGRAPHS, NO. 11
INSTITUTE OF LATIN AMERICAN STUDIES
THE UNIVERSITY OF TEXAS

ORIGINS OF THE AMERICAN INDIANS

European Concepts, 1492-1729

By Lee Eldridge Huddleston

PUBLISHED FOR THE INSTITUTE OF LATIN AMERICAN STUDIES
BY THE UNIVERSITY OF TEXAS PRESS, AUSTIN AND LONDON

Standard Book Number 292–73693–2
Library of Congress Catalog Card Number 67–65582
Copyright © 1967 by Lee Eldridge Huddleston

Manufactured in the United States of America
Second Printing, 1970

PREFACE

This study grew out of a long-standing interest in the antiquity of man in America and a curiosity about the attitudes of the earliest Europeans in America concerning the problem of the origin of man in the New World. Because of the unitary traditions of the Christian church with respect to human origins, the Europeans automatically assumed that the American Indians derived from some Old World group. But certain questions remained: How did the natives get to the New World? When did they arrive? Did they bring their civilizations with them or develop them after their arrival? From what known group of people were they descended?

When I attempted to trace these points through the modern literature, I discovered that few writers showed a knowledge of, or any great interest in, the opinions of the men who wrote on this subject in the first two centuries of the European experience in America. The most frequently-quoted works dealing with the history of the opinions concerning the origins and antiquity of man in America (Winsor, 1889; Bancroft, 1886; Imbelloni, 1956) devoted only a few brief paragraphs to the sixteenth and seventeenth centuries. All the writers on this subject knew of the controversy between Hugo Grotius and Joannes de Laet in 1643–1644 (largely because of the reputation of Grotius), but none revealed any understanding of the intellectual or historiographical framework within which this controversy took place.

In addition to the Grotius-De Laet affair most modern writers knew of Gregorio García's *Origen de los indios* published in 1607, but few had actually used the book. Those authors who did refer to García used the 1729 edition which had been considerably expanded by Andres Barcia. I was struck by the fact that several authors who used García credited him with opinions inconsistent with other opinions attributed to him, and none of them matched my own reading of García. In a similar fashion other historiographical landmarks in the discussion of the origins of the Indians seemed either incorrectly or irrelevantly presented in the "standard" accounts.

My original intention was to investigate the literature of the sixteenth and seventeenth centuries to discover what were the opinions of Europeans of that period, how those opinions were derived, and how they changed. In the light of this investigation I have distinguished two rival, but not mutually exclusive, traditions in the origin literature. The Acostan Tradition, characterized by a moderate skepticism with respect to the comparative and exegetical methodology of the day, by an adherence to geographical and faunal considerations in theorizing, and by a reluctance to produce finished origin theories, is named for Joseph de Acosta, who gave the tradition its earliest extended example in the *Historia natural y moral de las Indias* in 1589/90. The Garcían Tradition, named for the author of the *Origen de los indios* (1607/1729), is marked by an uncritical acceptance of the comparative ethnological technique of determining origins and a tendency to accept trans-Atlantic migrations.

I chose to conclude this study in 1729 because the *Origen de los indios* was republished in that year; moreover, developments in comparative anatomy and biology and explorations in the Bering Strait region after 1729 placed the discussion of American Indians on a more nearly scientific level, and, finally, because the period after 1729 has not suffered the degree of neglect that marked the period before 1729.

It is a pleasure to acknowledge all those who aided me in the completion of this study, especially Professor Thomas F. McGann, of The University of Texas, for his support and his valuable criticisms of the text and Dr. Nettie Lee Benson, Librarian of the Latin-American Collection of The University of Texas, for her assistance in helping me to acquire and use rare materials. I would like also to thank Professors Thomas McKern, Michael G. Hall, and Warren Dean, of The University of Texas; Alice Benfer, of Austin, Texas, and Robert McAhren, of Washington and Lee College. To my students, who suffered through the completion of this essay with a minimum of complaint, I owe a note of appreciation.

Lee Huddleston

North Texas State University

CONTENTS

Preface vii

INTRODUCTION: The Discovery of the American Indian . 3

CHAPTER I: The Early Origin Literature, Oviedo to Acosta . 14

Beginnings of the Origin Literature, 1535–1540 . . 14

Expansion of the Argument, 1540–1580 21

The Ten Lost Tribes of Israel and the Ophirites . . . 33

CHAPTER II: Acosta and García, 1589–1607 48

Joseph de Acosta and the Acostan Tradition . . . 48

Gregorio García and the Garcían Tradition . . . 60

CHAPTER III: Spanish Scholarship after García, 1607–1729 . 77

CHAPTER IV: The Debate on the Origins
of the Indians in Northern Europe 110

Expansion of the Debate to Northern Europe, 1600–1640 . 110

The Grotius–De Laet Controversy 118

The Jews in America and The Hope of Israel, 1644–1660 . 128

Toward New Criteria: La Peyrère and the Pre-Adamites . 138

General Conclusions 144

Bibliography 149

Index 173

ORIGINS OF THE AMERICAN INDIANS

European Concepts, 1492–1729

The Discovery of the American Indian

W HEN COLUMBUS RETURNED to Europe in late 1492 he wrote a letter to his patrons Ferdinand and Isabella informing them of his discoveries in the Western Sea. He told them of the islands, the plants, the animals, and the people he had encountered there: "The people of this island Española and all the other islands which I have found and of which I have information, all go naked, although some of the women cover a single place with a leaf of a plant or with a net of cotton (Colón, 1960b:192)." This letter was subsequently published and went through several editions in various languages before the end of the century. Many Europeans received their first information on the New World from this letter; but it was singularly uninformative about the nature of the inhabitants:

They do not hold any creed nor are they idolaters, but they all believe that power and good are in the heavens and were very firmly convinced that I, with these ships and men, came from the heavens, and in this belief they everywhere received me after they had mastered their fear. This belief is not the result of ignorance, for they are, on the contrary, of a very acute intelligence and they are men who navigate all those seas, so that it is amazing how good an account they give of everything. It is because they have never seen people clothed or ships of such a kind . . . In all these islands, I saw no great diversity in the appearance of the people or in their manners and language. On the contrary they all understand one another (Colón, 1960*b*: 196–197).

In none of these statements did Columbus indicate any surprise at the presence of men in the lands he found. Nor is there any evidence of such concern in the remnants of his journal. His first comments on the Indians appear under the date October 11, 1492, in what Las Casas (whose notes on the journal are all that remain of it) says to be the Admiral's own words. Columbus described the Indians as "very friendly," with short, coarse hair "like that of a horse's tail," and of good stature. Columbus (1960*a*:24–25) also noted under the date October 13, 1492, that "their eyes were large and beautiful" and that "they are not at all black, but the color of the Canarians, and nothing else could be expected, since this is in one line from east to west with the island of Hierro in the Canaries."

There is no reason to expect Columbus to puzzle over the presence of men in the newly discovered lands. As is clear from a reading of his first letter (1960*b*) and his *Journal* (1960*a*), Columbus thought he had discovered some islands off the coast of Cathay; thus, he had no reason to wonder where the inhabitants could have come from. Later writers made much of the belief that Columbus identified Española with the Ophir of Solomon. This belief stems from Pedro Martir de Anglería's *Décadas* (1944:29): "This island of Española, which he affirmed to be the Ophir of which the third book of Kings speaks [RSV: II Chron. 8:18] . . ." Whether Columbus actually made such an identification or not is of little importance. The belief that he had done so was widespread and influenced subsequent writers who wished to locate Ophir in the West Indies.

It should be noted, however, that for Columbus to locate Ophir in the Indies in 1492 would not have the same implications as a similar placement by Cabello Valboa in 1580. In Columbus' time most writers thought Ophir to be in the Indies of Asia, and Columbus' identification of Española as Ophir did not take Ophir out of Asia. To make the same identification after 1522 would require a conscious break with tradition and elaborate reasons for placing Ophir in an unknown section of the world.

Columbus did not question the existence of men in the New World because he did not know it was a New World. The realization of this fact was a gradual one not fully made until the reports of the Magellan Expedition of 1519–1521 became available. There was, therefore, no reason to marvel at a New World filled with New Men because neither phenomenon was recognized as such. The first must be understood before the second could be considered.

A generation passed between the discovery and the identification of America as a New World. In the interim numerous accounts of the "Indies" appeared in Europe but few revealed any great concern for the population of the new-found lands. Vaz de Caminha of Cabral's expedition devoted only a brief section of his report to the natives of Brazil (Greenlee, 1938:10–11), and subsequent comments in Columbus' *Journal* revealed no growing concern for the inhabitants.

Amerigo Vespucci did such a good job of popularizing the New World in Europe that many northern Europeans agreed with the British poet-dramatist John Rastell (1848:31–32) when he wrote in 1520 that the Indies "Ben callyd America by cause only Americus dyd furst them fynde." Leaving aside for the moment the question of what Vespucci meant by the phrase "Mundus Novus," his writings reveal no comprehension that a new world of the type America proved to be would pose serious problems about the origin of its inhabitants—how did they get to the New World? where did they come from? and from what people were they descended?

Vespucci's comments on the population of the New World were very brief and almost totally uninformative. In his first published letter (July 18, 1500) he reported that the Indians were beardless, brown, naked, and cannibal, and that they had various languages (1951:276, 278, 281). At this time, however, Vespucci (1951:277) still believed the New World to be "bounded by the eastern parts of Asia . . . because . . . we saw divers animals, such as lions, stags, goats . . . which are not found on islands, but only on the mainland."

In his Lisbon letter (1951:290–292) Vespucci described the natives of Brazil as cruel and warlike, and ignorant of law, religion, rulers, immortality of the soul, and private property. By 1503 Vespucci had seen so much of the coast of America (from southern Argentina to the

Carolinas) that he had become convinced that it could not be Asia. Consequently, when he prepared his essay on the new lands, he chose to give it the title *Mundus Novus*—New World.

Later writers have taken Vespucci's use of the phrase *mundus novus* to indicate that Vespucci guessed that America was a distinct geographical entity, different from Asia, Europe, and Africa. A careful reading of Vespucci does not clearly indicate that that was what he had in mind. Considering the general concept of "worlds" in those days, it may well be that he chose to call America *Mundus Novus* to indicate that the "world" he was describing was unknown to the ancients (1951:299).

Vespucci's last letter (1506) does not clarify his meaning in *Mundus Novus,* but it does contribute a few more elements to his description of the Indians. They were reddish, but he thought they would be white were they not constantly exposed to the sun (1951:311). Vespucci continued with the assertion that "they have broad faces, so that their appearance may be that of the Tartar" (1951:311). This appears to be the earliest comparison of the Indians with the Tatars, a practice which would become exceedingly frequent in the future. But it would be improper to postulate that Vespucci imagined a Tatar origin for the American Indians. His intent probably was merely descriptive.

It seems likely that Vespucci did not suspect the true geographical relationship of America to Asia. He was certain that America was not the Asia of the travelers—such as John of Carpini or the Polos—or of the Portuguese navigators; but he appears to have retained his belief that America was "bounded by the eastern parts of Asia." This would explain why it never occurred to him, in print at least, to wonder how the Indians got to the New World.

The recognition that the presence of the Indian in the New World did pose a problem begins to emerge in the works of Pedro Martir de Anglería, who completed and published the first book of his *Décadas del Nuevo Mundo* in 1511. Two additional books followed in 1516, a fourth in 1521, and the rest of the work by 1530. In the composition of his work Anglería relied heavily on firsthand reports from *conquistadores*. Among his informants was Martín Fernández de Enciso, an important figure in the conquest of Darién, and a major enemy of

Balboa. Fernández de Enciso wrote his own *Suma de geografía que trata de todas las partidas y provincias del mundo: en especial de las Indias* (1519), which contained little of importance on the West Indies (1530:fol. 50v–58). The volume was later translated into English and presented to Henry VIII as Roger Barlow's *Summe of Geographie* (Fernández de Enciso, 1897:v–viii; Barlow, 1932:xiii–xv).

Anglería's *Décadas* proved popular. The original editions were issued in Latin. The first "Decade" was translated into German (1534), English (1555), Dutch (1563), and Italian (1564). The second and third appeared in French (1532) and English (1555). The entire work appeared in English in abridged form in 1577, and in complete form in 1607. The 1607 English translation was made from a French translation of 1587. The *Décadas* did not appear in Spanish until 1892.

Anglería's history was largely narrative and chronological; but he occasionally offered opinions on contested matters. In at least two instances he referred to the supposition that Solomon's Ophir was located in the Indies: once in claiming that Columbus identified Española as Ophir and again in suggesting (1944:50) that Solomon sent his ships to Española. In neither case did Anglería indicate that he thought Solomon's crew might have left behind a nucleus of people who could have produced the American Indians.

Later, in reporting the discovery by Columbus of fair-skinned youths near the equator, Anglería attributed this fairness in latitudes normally inhabited by dark-skinned peoples to the curvature of the earth which placed the people nearer to heaven (i.e., higher in altitude) thus negating the effects of the sun (1944:65–70). Later still Anglería attributed to Pinzón a comparison of some Indians to the Scythians—they were "nomads like the Scythians" (1944:91). Returning to Pinzón much later, Anglería recounted the story of a contact between Pinzón and some Indians of Paria in 1514. The Parians presented the Spanish with a barrel of incense, which led Pinzón to conclude that incense must grow in Paria since "the natives of Paria have no communication with the Sabeos [a people of southwestern Arabia], as they know absolutely nothing beyond their beaches" (1944:173).

Only once did Anglería point out contacts of non-Americans with the Indians which might have left a permanent population. In discuss-

ing Balboa's encounter with some Negroes on the Atlantic coast of
Panama, he attributed to Balboa the postulate that an Ethiopian raid-
ing party was shipwrecked in Panama, thus accounting for the Negroes
now there (1944:200). Peter Martyr also reported the practice of
circumcision in Yucatán which the Indians attributed to a former visi-
tor (1944:308–309). He did not, however, say he thought this might
indicate a Jewish origin for the Yucatecan Indians.

Anglería did not consider the question how the natives got to America, or from whom they descended. The first complete edition of the
Décadas appeared nine years after the return of the Magellan voyage,
and Anglería, who died in 1526 five years after the Pacific voyagers
returned, should have been aware of the difficulties involved in an
assumption that the Indians had come from Asia. Yet, despite the great
width of the Pacific, he does not appear to have grasped the seriousness
of the difficulties.

It was left to the English poet-dramatist John Rastell to ask the
question in print, in his *A New Interlude and a mery, of the nature of
the iiij Elements* (London, ca. 1520):

> And what a great and meritoryouse dede
> It were to have the people instructed
> To lyve more Vertuously
> And to lerne to knowe of man the maner
> And also to knowe of god theyr maker
> Which as yet lyve all bestly
> For they nother know god nor the devell
> Nor never harde tell of hevyn nor hell
> Wrytynge, nor other scripture:
> But yet in the stede of god almyght
> The honour the sone for his great lyggt
> For that doth them great pleasure. . . .
> But howe the people furst began
> In that countrey or whens they cam
> For clerkes it is a questyon (1848:29–31).

It is probable that none of the men who carried the burden of the
discussion of the problem of Indian origins ever read Rastell. Nor was
that necessary. The problem was one which would readily occur to men

of the early sixteenth century. So long as America was thought to be a part of Asia, or at least near it, it appears that Europeans automatically assumed that the inhabitants of the New World were of Asiatic derivation. But, when the growing evidence, capped by the Magellan expedition, proved that the known parts of America were farther from Asia than from Europe this neat explanation of the presence of men in America was no longer tenable. It was almost universally believed in Europe in the early sixteenth century that all men were derived primarily from Adam and Eve, and secondarily from Noah and the other survivors of the Flood. Animals as well as men could be traced to Noah's Ark; and all men and animals in the world, despite their present locations, *must* be traced to the Ark.

Tradition had it that Eden, the original home of man, was somewhere in the Near East. There was some dispute over its precise location, but the consensus was definitely in favor of Mesopotamia (Williams, 1948:94–111; Raleigh, 1820:I, 71–140). But the exact location did not become an important factor in tracing the first men in America until the twentieth century. What was most important to the early commentators on the subject of Indian origins was the location of the landing place of the Ark. Here again, tradition favored the Near East—Armenia; and since only eight humans survived the Flood, all modern peoples had to be traced to those eight and to Armenia (Hodgen, 1964:207–253).

It was not difficult to understand how the children of the Ark could multiply and spread over the continents of Asia, Africa, and Europe, inasmuch as these continents were all part of one great land mass. It was also easy to comprehend that the islands adjacent to the continents could likewise be filled with men, since Noah no doubt passed the art of navigation along to his children and grandchildren. Renaissance man likewise readily understood that animals could spread over the Afro-Eurasian land mass with little trouble. They thought also that the nearby islands could be inhabited by animals who swam there, or were carried there by men for their own purposes.

But how did men get to America? When did they go? From what part of the Old World had they departed? And from what known people were they descended? Writers did not credit the statement attributed to Paracelsus that maybe God had created a second Adam for America (Bendyshe, 1865–67:353–355). These questions, addressed originally to the problem posed by man's presence in a genuine New World, must eventually be applied to the animals also; for they, no less than men, were children of the Ark. These considerations became current in the literature on America in the 1530's. Few books printed after that date were able to avoid a review of these problems. Many of them include at least a few pages offering solutions to the questions. But few writers accepted without modification the views of others.

By 1530 the seriousness of the problem posed by the presence of men in the New World was only partly comprehended. For the most part the American Indian dominated the debate; the question of the animals entered the theorizing near the end of the sixteenth century. The period from about 1530 to 1607 was characterized by brief and simplistic solutions. The only important exception was the comprehensive review of all phases of the matter by Joseph de Acosta in 1589/90 and a few unpublished works of the 1580's. In 1607 the great importance of the questions at hand was pointed up by the publication of the first book devoted exclusively to the subject of American origins. The first edition of Gregoria García's *Origen de los indios de el nuevo mundo* appeared in that year. In the one hundred and twenty-two years separating the first and second editions of that book the debate involved a few of the greatest minds in Europe and became an integral part of such problems as the theological discussion of the universality of the Flood, the readmission of the Jews to England, the legitimacy of European national claims to the Indies, and various scientific and esoteric matters. *Origen de los indios* was republished in 1729 with considerable additions by Andrés Gonzales de Barcia Carballido y Zúñiga. Barcia's additions increased the size of the volume by perhaps a quarter, but they consisted of bibliographical entries and summaries of later opinions.

The first two hundred years of investigation into the problems raised by the existence of unknown men in America show a remarkable unity despite the fantastic variety of solutions suggested. The methodology utilized by a majority of the writers was essentially deductive and exegetical, with minimum reliance on or even recognition of experience as a factor. Yet at the same time there was a persistent theme of skepticism and caution running through the thinking of several writers.

As in most cases of controversy in this period, the question of Indian origins was limited by the necessity to conform to Christian theology. Some writers spent much of their time on the subject analyzing the various passages of the Scriptures which could conceivably be related to the matter. Sometimes the proffered solution would rely wholly on evidences and deductions from biblical literature. Alternately, an author might offer a solution derived from accepted ancient authorities. Many writers freely mixed ancient and scriptural references. The latter practice was probably typical.

As Arnold Williams adequately indicated in his study of the commentaries on Genesis in the sixteenth and seventeenth centuries (1948: 3–24), most Europeans did not distinguish between the Bible and the traditional interpretations associated with it. Many men active in the debate on Indian origins drew much of their knowledge of ancient texts from the scriptural commentaries rather than from the texts themselves.

At no time in the period before 1729 did anyone offer an origin theory which could not be made consistent with the Bible. Sometimes, as in the case of Isaac de la Peyrère and his postulate of the existence of man before Adam, the rationalization was openly contrary to accepted tradition; but La Peyrère made the effort.

Experience was at no time denied, not even by the most credulous writers. From the earliest days of the sixteenth century, writers on America recognized that the experiences of the generation of the Conquest refuted many of the classical authorities—notably Aristotle, St. Augustine, and others who had argued that man could not live in the "Burning Zone," nor cross it to inhabit any possible southern continent, or Antipodes. Here was an obvious instance where Europeans could recognize "that it is certain, that practice is of more value than theory" (Vespucci, 1951:276). Acosta (1940), as well as several others, spent much of the early parts of his *Historia natural y moral de las Indias* disproving Aristotle and St. Augustine with references to recent experiences (Hornberger, 1939).

There was no sweeping rejection of authority. In those instances where experience obviously contradicted the ancients, the ancients were indeed rejected. But this rejection was particular rather than general. Throughout the two centuries the tendency was to accept the testimony of the ancient authorities except in those areas specifically contradicted by experience. The result was a curious mixture of observation and obscurantism especially prevalent in the sixteenth century and continuing throughout the period. In parts of Europe—notably in Holland and England—and in certain individual cases, the emphasis began to shift away from overreliance on authority toward a greater adherence to experience and to arguments drawn from natural science. Late in the seventeenth century the French naturalists began to show an interest in the origins of the Indians, and the debate began to take on a distinctly nontheological character although it never shed all its theological elements.

This essay concerns the debate over the origins of the American Indians in the two centuries before it became distinguished from the question of the origins of their cultures, and before it began to take on the characteristics of a scientific dispute. In the period from 1492 to 1729 the problem of Indian origins was indistinct from the general problem of human origins. The highly restricted time scheme accepted by Europeans in those days did not allow a separation of the two. The time between the Deluge and 1500 covered at most some 4000 years (Allen, 1948:84–87). That was little enough time to allow men to reach their historic locations. Polygenism, the belief in multiple origins for men, though attributed to Paracelsus in 1520 and definitely supported by La Peyrère in 1655, was not seriously considered until the late nineteenth century.

The age conceived the question of human, and therefore Indian, origins as largely theological. But many nontheological considerations were apparent from the beginning and gradually increased in importance throughout the period. Nonetheless, these extra-theological considerations—geography, ethnology, and faunal distribution—operated within limits imposed by theology. Given the common derivation of all men, and the brief time of man on earth, a large measure of cultural conformity between widely separated tribal groups must be assumed.

Consequently, the method for discovering the origins of an isolated tribe consisted of tracing its cultural affinities with known peoples. Most writers of the period assumed that close cultural similarities indicated a common ancestry. This method dominated the entire first two centuries, but not without considerable questioning as to its validity (Hodgen, 1964:254–353; Allen, 1949:113–137).

Two clearly distinguished traditions have emerged from my investigations: the Acostan and the Garcían. The first, marked by a skepticism with regard to cultural comparisons, considerable restraint in constructing theories, and a great reliance on geographical and faunal considerations, is named for Joseph de Acosta, who gave it its earliest clear expression in his *Historia natural y moral* of 1589/1590. The Garcían Tradition, named for the author of the *Origen de los indios* (1607), is characterized by a strong adherence to ethnological comparisons, a tendency to accept trans-Atlantic migrations, and an acceptance of *possible* origins as *probable* origins.

CHAPTER I

The Early Origin Literature, Oviedo to Acosta

Beginnings of the Origin Literature, 1535–1540

THE OCTOBER, 1965, issue of *American Antiquity*, the leading publication in the field of early American archæology, carried an article by Edwin N. Wilmsen on the history of the study of early man in America. In the brief space allotted to the pre-1780 period, and drawing largely from Justin Winsor's *Narrative and Critical History of America* (Boston, 1889), Wilmsen asserted that "perhaps the most favored view among the early Spanish settlers was that the Indians were not really human." He hinted that the popularity of the theory might be related to the Spanish desire to enslave the Indians (1965: 173).

This intriguing idea was not invented by Mr. Wilmsen. This writer has heard it in private conversations, in lectures, and student reports. The assumption that the early Spaniards thought the Indians somehow "nonhuman" is evidently widespread (De Camp, 1954:30). But so far as can be determined from the literature published at the time, the impression is a wholly false one. The source of such an impression is unclear, but it apparently stemmed from a misunderstanding of the controversy over the ability of the Indians to understand and accept the Christian faith, and their ability to reason. Early reports frequently charged that the natives of the New World were without recognizable creed or religion. Columbus had noted that a particular group of Indians "do not hold any creed"; but, he added immediately, "nor are they idolaters" (1960b:196). Vespucci also observed that the Indians of Brazil were ignorant of religion (1951:290).

The belief that the Indians were inferior to Europeans no doubt predominated; after all, the Indians did not live according to Christian ideas (Hanke, 1937:68–73). Yet, many writers specifically affirmed their belief that the Indians were descendants of Noah and as such must be capable of reason, though this fact might be obscured by their idolatrous practices (Oviedo, 1944–1945:III, 60). Most writers believed the Indians could become Christians. Such a belief was also implicit in the missionizing activities of the Church, and in the decree of Clement VII in 1530 authorizing the use of force in converting the natives (Harrisse, 1958:273). Paul III made it explicit in his bull *Sublimus Deus* of 1537 which states "that the Indians are truly men and are not only capable of understanding the catholic faith but . . . desire exceedingly to receive it" (Hanke, 1937:71–72).

Certain factors appear to lend credence to the assumption that there was a belief in the nonhuman character of the Indians. For one, the assertion in a papal bull that the Indians "are truly men" would appear to indicate that the point was in dispute. That implication, however, should not be greatly emphasized. The primary purpose of *Sublimus Deus,* other than the missionary objective, was to confirm the right of the Indians to possess property, thus preventing wholesale confiscation by the Spanish settlers. Paul affirmed that the Indians were "truly men" as part of his rationale for confirming their property rights (Hanke, 1937:71–74; 1959:1–27).

This interpretation is supported—though not definitively of course —by the absence of any literary exposition of the idea that the Indians were animals or creatures of the Devil rather than men. The writers appear not to have noticed such a possibility; few even questioned the ability of the Indians to reason. Therefore, although some men may have believed the Indians to be of nonhuman stock, the idea does not seem to have been seriously proposed.

The literary debate on the problems raised by the presence of men in the New World began in 1535 with the publication of the first part of Gonzalo Fernández de Oviedo y Valdéz' *Historia general y natural de las índias islas y Tierra Firme del Mar Océano* in Sevilla. Other men, such as Pedro Sancho, Francisco de Xerez, Cortés, and Miguel de Estete, had already written firsthand accounts of America. Their accounts were, however, concerned wholly with military and political developments; their comments on the Indians were of little ethnological value. Sancho, in a passage typical of much of the other works, stated in his *An Account of the Conquest of Peru* (1534) that "the people of this province, as well men as women, are very filthy, and they have large hands, and the province is very large" (1917:167). The reports of most of the conquistadores were similarly uninformative.

With Oviedo the pattern of comment changed. His purpose differed from that of previous writers in that it was historical. Columbus and Vespucci concerned themselves with description. Anglería produced a chronological narrative. The other commentators wrote largely for political and apologetical reasons. Oviedo brought good credentials to his task. He had traveled in the Caribbean region of America extensively and could therefore write with considerable firsthand knowledge. Furthermore, he had the writings of all other commentators on the American continent. Oviedo had already written a brief *Sumario de la natural historia de las Indias* in 1526. His *Historia general* was the result then of both personal experience and long acquaintance with the literature on America.

The complete *Historia general* was approximately twenty times the size of the *Sumario*. Only the first part was published in Oviedo's lifetime. The entire work finally appeared in 1851–1855 (4v., Madrid). The most recent edition (Asunción de Paraguay, 1944–1945) contains fourteen volumes. Since Oviedo proposed a synthesis of all available material on the New World and a consideration of all its problems, he had to consider the questions of who the first settlers were, and where they came from. The material on these points, which appeared in the volume published in 1535, constituted the first literary discussion of the subject.

Oviedo offered two opinions about the place of origin of the Indians. On the one hand he hinted that Carthage might be their ancestral home; on the other, he thought it most likely that the earliest inhabitants of the New World descended from the ancient Spaniards. Oviedo's Carthaginian story introduced into the origin literature the most persistent of all the trans-Atlantic origin theories. The story revolves around a statement attributed to Aristotle by one Theophilus de Ferrariis in his *Admirandis in natura auditis*. The work by Aristotle from which this story was taken, *Mirabilibus aut secultationibus*,* was not available to the men of the Renaissance except by way of Theophilus (Oviedo, 1944–1945:I, 45; Fernando Colón, 1947:57; Suárez de Peralta, 1949:5). Fernando Colón, who apparently knew the story from Greek as well as Latin sources, included a Spanish translation of his own in his biography of his father. Since the story recurred so frequently, a translation from Fernando follows:

> It is said that some Carthaginian merchants in ancient times found in the Atlantic beyond the Pillars of Hercules a certain island which had never been inhabited except by savage beasts. It was all forested, with many navigable rivers, and abounded in all things that nature produced. But it was many days sailing from the mainland. On arriving there, the Carthaginian merchants, seeing that the land was good because of its fertility and its temperate climate, settled down. But the Carthaginian Senate, angered by this, publicly decreed that no one could go to the island under pain of death. Those who had first gone were condemned to death in order that news of the island not reach other nations, and some stronger empire take possession of it and thus make it contrary to and inimical to the liberties of Carthage (1947:57).

Oviedo's version of the story differed only slightly and in unimportant ways. According to him the merchants went through the "Estrecho de Gibraltar," the island was *large,* and it had never been "discovered" before. He referred to "wild and other" beasts; spoke of "large" trees and "marvellous" rivers; elaborated on "the things that nature produced"; located the island with respect to Africa; elaborated on the settlement of the island; and referred to the potential "inconvenience" to the Carthaginians and to their liberties. Only in locating the island with respect to known continental areas did Oviedo introduce an ele-

---

* The title is given in Curzola (1943:28–29) as *De Mirabilibus auscultationibus*.

ment which could not readily be inferred from the version of Fernando (1944–1945:I, 45–46).

Oviedo stated that he thought Aristotle's story pictured conditions in Cuba or Española so well that he must have meant to describe them. He concluded that the Carthaginians had discovered the Indies long before Columbus arrived. Oviedo quoted Aristotle as saying "that those who had gone to the island they killed." Consequently, it is uncertain whether he thought some of the original settlers might have escaped to form a nucleus of the Indian population. Considering his later acceptance of an earlier discovery, that seems unlikely (1944–1945:I, 46).

Oviedo offered the Carthaginian story as a clue to the possible first discovery of America. But immediately thereafter he offered what he considered a far better theory. "I take these Indies to be those famous Islas Hespérides, so called after the twelfth king of Spain, Héspero" (1944–1945:I, 46). Oviedo derived his knowledge of the early kings of Spain from Berosus, a chronicler of questionable veracity (Oviedo, 1851–1855:I, 15, n.1). The gist of his argument was that during the reign of King Héspero (which began about 1658 B.C.) Spaniards discovered, peopled, and ruled the Indies. They named the Indies for their king—Islas Hespérides. These were the same islands as those of later Greek mythology. Sometime after the days of Héspero contact with the islands was broken, and they were forgotten except by the Greek mythmakers (1944–1945:I, 48). The author claimed, then, that the Indies were discovered by Spaniards over three thousand years before Columbus. Through the agency of Columbus, God had returned the Indies to their rightful owner—the Spanish crown (1944–1945: I, 51).

Oviedo's primary purpose in the chapter devoted to the first settlers was to reveal who had found America first. Settlement was incidental. Though he did not return to the question of Indian origins in the part published in 1535, there are, however, several references of interest to the discussion of origins in the material he did not publish. He specifically rejected the idea that America might be connected by land to some part of Europe or Asia in the unexplored north. By implication, then, Oviedo eliminated a land bridge as a means of getting the first settlers to the New World (1944–1945:III, 184–186; X, 287–289).

The impression with which the reader is left is that Oviedo intended to derive the total population of the New World from the "Hesperian" settlers. The Carthaginians may have added to the population at a later date.

Some Spaniards did not receive Oviedo's *Historia general y natural* favorably, and in later years several commentators took exception to his theories. One of the first literary consequences of the work was to spur Christopher Columbus' son Fernando to write a biography of his father —*Vida del Almirante Don Cristóbal Colón*—written largely to correct certain real and presumed errors respecting Christopher. The son was particularly incensed by Oviedo's attempt to rob his father of the glory of being the first discoverer of the New World. He completed the biography before 1539, but unfortunately he did not publish it. The book appeared first in an Italian translation in 1571. His arguments are, however, germane, and they illustrate the availability and types of information which could be turned against the Oviedo position (O'Gorman, 1951:80–82).

Fernando started his critique of Oviedo's Carthaginian and Hesperian theories by calling them fantasies, void of reason or foundation (1947:56–57). He then made a detailed analysis of each story. Fernando charged that much of Oviedo's trouble stemmed from the fact that he did not know Latin and had to rely on someone else's bad translation. He quoted the tale of Aristotle from a Greek version, and berated Oviedo for his errors. Fernando also pointed out that Aristotle himself had cast doubt on the validity of the story by beginning it with a word meaning "it is told," rather than claiming he had it on authority (1947:57–59).

The younger Columbus doubted the validity of the tale from internal evidence also. It did not seem reasonable to him that a land could be fertile if men were not around to cultivate it. Nor could he imagine the Carthaginian Senate disliking the discovery of so wonderful a place. If they wanted to prevent someone else from taking it over and making it a threat to Carthage, would it not have been more reasonable to settle it themselves rather than to attempt to suppress the discovery? After all, others might make the same discovery by accident as the Carthaginian merchants had. Even if the "fable" could be credited, the description did not fit either Cuba or Española, since neither had fierce beasts (1947:58–62).

Fernando turned immediately from the first theory to the second. He accused Oviedo of misrepresenting his sources when he used Hyginus to support his belief that the Hespérides lay in the western part of the Atlantic. Fernando was unfair in stressing this point. Oviedo mentioned Hyginus only once, and that was in a reference to Berosus (1851–1855:I, 17). According to Fernando, Hyginus mentioned the Hespérides only three times. Twice he placed the islands in the East; the other time he mentioned the ancient name of Venus—Hesperus. Thus, concluded Fernando, if the Indies were known as the Hespérides in ancient times Hyginus could only be used to argue that the name derived from Venus, the most prominent light in the western sky at sunset. Anyway, said Fernando, Oviedo could not with reason argue on the one hand that the ancient Spaniards settled the Indies, and then on the other accept the Carthaginian story that the island was undiscovered before the merchants arrived (1947:62–63).

Oviedo's argument for a Spanish origin for the inhabitants of the New World received little support, and was rarely mentioned. But the Carthaginian story, which he introduced but apparently did not accept, achieved great popularity. Oviedo did not develop the theory very far. Therefore, most of the later writers who accepted it relied not so much on Oviedo as on the writings of the well-known Spanish mystic Alejo Vanegas de Bustos. Vanegas expounded the Carthaginian origin theory in his *Primera Parte de las differencias de libros q̃ ay in el universo* (Toledo, 1540). The book went through four editions by 1583, but is now exceedingly rare. Fortunately, José Toribio Medina reprinted the pages relating to America in the first volume of his *Biblioteca Hispano-Americana* (1898:I, 162–165).

Vanegas clearly argued that the first inhabitants of America descended from Carthaginian settlers. He did not quote Aristotle's story. He stated merely that "it is obvious that the islands which Don Cristóbal Colón and Vespucio Amerigo [sic] discovered had already been found more than two thousand years ago," and that the Carthaginian settlers in the islands spread to the mainland and populated it. Nor, said he (1898:164), should we wonder at that, for "if Adam and Eve populated the three parts of the world, why marvel that the Phoenicians and Carthaginians could populate America which was a neighbor to the islands of Española and Cuba?"

Vanegas, like Oviedo, explicitly included the Indians among the descendants of Noah. But he went further than Oviedo and used that fact as an argument to prove that the Indies must have been discovered before Columbus, since there were men there before Columbus arrived. Since Aristotle's Carthaginian story was available, Vanegas used it to explain the earliest discovery and settlement of America. In doing so he was either ignorant of, or at least ignored, the fact that Aristotle had said the men who went to the "island" were condemned to death (with the apparent implication that they were executed) and knowledge of the discovery suppressed.

Vanegas may have known of Oviedo's *Historia general y natural,* but he did not refer to it. The stories of Aristotle were common knowledge among the educated classes of Spain, and the use of them to explain the origins of the Indians would readily occur to a man who had seen the great trans-Atlantic migration of the Spanish in the early sixteenth century.

Expansion of the Argument, 1540–1580

Most books about the origins of the American Indians assume that Europeans began to wonder about the problem immediately after learning about the discovery. That assumption is probably correct, but literary evidence of any great controversy or puzzlement over Indian origins is slight before 1550. Only two theories seem to have appeared in that period. No doubt others were discussed, but except for Oviedo and Vanegas they did not reach the printed page. Neither of the two referred to any contemporary commentators on the subject.

The most vital questions concerning the Indians did not deal with their origins or how they got to the New World. The questions focused on whether the Indians were capable of becoming Christians; whether they should be converted peacefully or forcibly; whether they were rational beings possessed of the rights of Europeans; whether they should be enslaved, or, if already slave, liberated (Hanke, 1959). The issue of the *nature* and *use* of the Indians came to a climax in the New Laws of the 1540's with first a victory then a defeat for the humanitarians. The question of the Indian's nature *could* have a relation to the question of his origin, since Europeans were likely to view Indians descended from Spaniards differently from Indians descended from Jews, Carthaginians, or Ethiopians. The men involved in the controversy apparently did not make such connections.

The influence of the materials on the debate over the nature of the Americans on the public debate on origins was slight, except to the extent that they illustrate something of the intellectual background in which the authors of the origin literature worked. After 1550 the interest in the inhabitants of the New World and a mushrooming interest in America in general let loose a torrent of books on the new-found lands. A substantial number of these works included a consideration of the possible sources of the American population. The majority, however, ignored such problems and concentrated on telling a good story.

The most famous of the Spanish humanitarians, Bartolomé de Las Casas, wrote on the origins of the Indians in two works not published in his lifetime: the *Apologética historia,* completed by 1550, and his *Historia de las Indias,* completed by 1559. Since these books were first published in 1909 and 1875–1876 respectively, they did not contribute directly to the literary debate. Two reasons favor their inclusion: they are illustrative of the thinking of one of the men intimately involved with the condition of the Indian, and they indicate that Las Casas did not hold an opinion commonly attributed to him—that the Indians descended from the Lost Ten Tribes of Israel.

In his *Apologética historia* Las Casas stated that he believed that the Indians of the Western Indies descended from those of the East Indies because the "West Indies are part of the East Indies." He based this conclusion on a comparison of "the multitude of peoples and nations and diverse languages" which were characteristic of the West Indies and also, according to Herodotus and Diodorus, of East India (1909: 53–54).

Las Casas spent most of his time in the *Apologetic History* proving the worth and religiosity of the Indians. He did, however, return to the origin question near the end of the volume to make an extended criticism of the use of language comparisons as evidence of origin. He referred to some anonymous "Doctor" (probably a misunderstanding of Anglería) who connected the practice of circumcision and the presence of a few words resembling Hebrew in Yucatán to postulate a Judaic origin for the Yucatecan Indians. Las Casas laughingly pointed out that such comparisons could also prove that the Indians came from Italy, from the village of Batea in Cataluña, from Baeza in Castilla, from Greece or Spain in general, or from any of the Arab lands. Most American languages, he noted, have certain words which resemble one or more Old World tongues (1909:632–649). This seems to refute those (Simon, 1836:3–5; Torquemada, 1723:24) who attribute a Jewish origin theory to Las Casas.

Las Casas returned to the question of Indian origins in his *Historia de las Indias*. He carefully evaluated the traditions and legends of land in the Western Ocean and their influence on Columbus. Most of them he classified as fables. He did, however, accept the prior existence of Atlantis; but he did not postulate it as a possible source of the natives of America (1951:I, 49–54). He examined the Carthaginian story as told by Aristotle and rejected it as of dubious value (1951:I, 55–56). Las Casas then turned his attention to Oviedo and his theory of a Spanish origin for the earliest Americans. Borrowing heavily from Fernando Colón's manuscript biography of the Admiral, Las Casas disputed with Oviedo at length, then rejected it as improbable, fictitious, and frivolous (1951:I, 73–90). He likewise rejected the identification of Española or any other American area with the biblical Ophir; Ophir, he argued, was in East Asia (1951:I, 53, 487–489).

On the whole Las Casas was noncommittal about who the Indians were or where or how they had come to the New World. The *Historia de las Indias* contains no affirmation of the East Indian origin he had presumed in the *Apologética historia* of 1550. It was as if Las Casas on reflection had decided that the problem was genuinely beyond solution because the Indians had come to America so long ago their route could not be traced. Las Casas recorded a curious story in the *Historia* which tends to support this conclusion:

I have seen in these mines of Cibao, a *stadia* or two deep in the virgin earth, in the plains at the foot of some hills, burned wood and ashes as if a few days ago a fire was made there. And for the same reason we have to conclude that in other times the river came near there, and in that place they made a fire, and afterwards the river went away. The soil brought from the hills by the rains covered it [the fire site]. And because this could not happen except by the passage of many years and most ancient time, there is a great argument that the people of these islands and continent are very ancient (1951:I, 375).

Las Casas did not pursue this line of thought. But the implications of even so brief a statement are staggering. Two hundred years would pass before such distinctively archæological thinking would reenter the search for clues to the antiquity and origins of the American Indians. Steno's exposition on index fossils in geology did not appear until 1669. It is tantalizing to speculate on the possible results had Las Casas recognized the scientific potential of his observation and elaborated upon it; or the possible consequences had he published it in 1559.

One of Las Casas' greatest enemies in his battle for humanitarian treatment for the Indians, Francisco López de Gómara, the secretary and biographer of Hernando Cortés, contributed to the debate. In 1552 López de Gómara published his *Historia general de las Indias* at Zaragoza. The book consisted of two parts: a "General History" and a "Chronicle of New Spain," which was essentially a biography of Cortés. Six editions of the book appeared before 1554, but it ran into considerable difficulty. The author despised the Indians and filled his volume with outrageous characterizations of them. He stated (1941:66–72) that their principal god was the devil; that they engaged in public sexual intercourse like animals, and were "the greatest sodomists"; that they were liars, ingrates, and the source of syphilis. He further contended that many were cannibals and knew nothing of justice; that they went shamelessly nude; that they "are like stupid, wild, insensate asses," prone to "novelties," drunkenness, vice, and fickleness; that, in short, they were the worst people God ever made. López de Gómara wrote his book in part "to persuade [the Council of the Indies] that they do not deserve liberty" and, consequently, decided they should be enslaved (1941:II, 242–244).

Las Casas bitterly resented these slanders on the Indians' character and strongly opposed the book, saying its author had never even visited America but merely wrote what Cortés told him to write. Las Casas' influence was sufficient to convince Prince Philip to suppress the book in late 1553.

López de Gómara made a considerable contribution to the literature on origins. Not only did he stimulate thinking and response by his treatment of the Indians, but he also stirred up controversies by claiming a pre-Columbian discovery of America by an "anonymous pilot" who, Gómara claimed, told Columbus about his find. The chronicler deprecated also the role of everyone but Cortés in the conquest of Mexico (1941:I, 37–38). He appears, moreover, to have been the first author to suggest Atlantis as a possible source for the aborigines of the Indies. His reasoning was that the Mexican Indians used the word "atl" for water and that they derived this word from memories of their ancient homeland, Atlantis, now sunk beneath the waters of the ocean (1941:II, 248–249).

López de Gómara did not insist that Atlantis was the sole origin of the Indians. He conceded that ancients other than Plato knew of America and that their knowledge might indicate a migration to America other than the Atlantean. He suggested (1941:II, 248) that Seneca might have meant America when he wrote in his tragedy *Medea,*

> An age shall come, ere ages ende,
> Blessedly strange and strangely blest,
> When our Sea farre and neare or'prest,
> His shoare shall yet extend.
>
> Descryed then shall a large Land be,
> By this profound Seas navigation,
> An other World, an other nation,
> All Men shall then discovered see.
>
> Thule accounted heretofore
> The worldes extreme, the Northern bound,
> Shall be when Southwest parts be found,
> A neerer Isle, a neighbor shoare.
>
> (from Edward Grimston's 1604
> translation of Acosta, 1963:34)

There is a crucial difference between the English translation and the Latin and Spanish versions presented by Las Casas, Acosta, and García: The Latin version as given by Las Casas (1957–1961:I, 42) and García (1729:24–25) read

> Venient annis
> Secula seris, quibus Oceanus
> Vincula rerum laxet et ingens
> Pateat telus Tethysque novos
> Detegat orbes nec sit terris*
> Ultima Thule.

*[*terrarum* in Las Casas]

The Spanish version provided by Acosta (1962:37–38) and García (1729:24–25) agrees with the English translation in the first and third stanzas, but the second stanza, as with lines four and five of the Latin, differs from the English.

> Descubriran grande tierra
> verán otro Nueva Mundo
> navegando el gran profundo*
> que agora el paso nos cierra.

*[*Mar profundo* in García]

Spanish writers who referred to Seneca understood him to mean "an other New World," rather than merely "an other world." Since America was commonly called the New World, this translation gave a slightly stronger argument to those who held that the ancients knew of America.

López de Gómara thought that the Carthaginian Hanno might have visited Cuba or Española (1941:II, 249). He cited one theory which he did not think valid. According to this theory, some Spaniards left Spain to settle the Indies after the defeat of the Gothic armies by the Muslims in 711 A.D. (1941:I, 115).

The tempo of the discussion increased rapidly after López de Gómara entered the field. Whereas there were no new theories expounded in the 1540's, if one excepts Vanegas' elaboration of the Carthaginian story, there were few years after 1552 when new accounts did not appear. Pedro Cieza de León announced in the *Primera parte de la crónica del Perú* (Sevilla, 1553) that he intended to discuss the Deluge and the origins of the Indians in Chapter III of the second part (1941: 291). When part two did appear in 1873, the promised discussion existed only as an uninformative fragment. Also in 1553 Florián de Ocampo published his *Los cinco primeros libros de la Corónica general de España* at Alcalá. In that volume Ocampo hinted that Hanno the Carthaginian might have visited Española, presumably leaving some settlers there (1776:fol. cl–cli).

The year 1555 marked the entry of non-Spaniards into the discussion of Indian origins for the first time since John Rastell had asked the question about "whens they cam." In that year the Englishman Richard Eden issued at London a translation of the first four books of Pedro Martir de Anglería's *Décadas* and sections of Oviedo's *Historia general y natural*. A second edition of Eden's translation, with the last four books of the *Decades* translated by Richard Willes, appeared in abridged form in 1577. In his introduction to the English reader Eden made the rather puzzling assertion "that since the creation of the world untyll the yeare before named, there hath byn no passage from our knowen partes of the world to these newe landes" (1885:51). Eden alluded also to the Indians having lived under "Sathan tyrannie," and asserted that they had souls. It would appear that Eden rejected the possibility of a trans-Atlantic migration into America; but he gave no indication whence the Indians may have come.

The other non-Spaniard whose work appeared in 1555 was the Portuguese Antonio Galvão. His *Tratado* was translated into English by Richard Hakluyt as *The Discoveries of the World, from their first Original Unto the Year of Our Lord 1555* (London, 1601). The first edition, and the second of 1563, are extremely rare; but the Hakluyt translation, and a corrected translation published together with the 1563 edition are available.

Galvão spent several years in the Orient as governor of the Portuguese island of Ternaté in the Moluccas. While there he heard of a Chinese tradition claiming that voyagers from China had populated the New World. Galvão considered this very plausible, because both Chinese and Indians had similar—but unspecified—"fashions and cus-

toms" and because their "small eies, flat noses," and other physical
characteristics were similar (1862:19). Galvão also knew of Oviedo's
work, and he recounted the tale of the Carthaginian discovery. He sar-
castically pointed out that those who once postulated a pre-Columbian
discovery of the Antilles were now doing the same thing for New
Spain (1862:34).

The Spaniard Agustín de Zárate published his *Historia del descubrimiento y conquista de la provincia del Perú* at Anvers in 1555. The
book proved amazingly popular. Spanish editions followed in 1560
and 1577; an Italian translation appeared in 1563, one in German in
1564, in French in 1570, and in English in 1581. Zárate offered only
one theory—an elaboration on the Atlantean theory of López de Gómara. Zárate thought that the customs of the Atlanteans as described by
Plato were still preserved in Peru. He concluded, then, that people
from Atlantis migrated to America before Atlantis sank into the ocean
(Zárate, n.d.:505–508).

Over the next few years several writers contributed to the general
discussion by elaborating arguments already current. Francisco Cervantes de Salazar accepted Zárate's argument for Atlantis when he
wrote his *Crónica de la Nueva España* around 1560. The book was not
published until 1914, but it was used in manuscript by Antonio de
Herrera in the early seventeenth century and by Andrés Barcia in 1729
(Cervantes de Salazar, 1914:4–7). Another of the lesser writers was
Giralmo Benzoni, whose popular *L'Istoria del mondo Nuovo* (Venice,
1565) appeared in French, Latin, German, and Flemish translations
before 1600. Benzoni accepted the story of the Carthaginian merchants
out of Aristotle, thus continuing and strengthening a vital tradition. It
should be noted, however, that Benzoni (1857:15) did not unreserv-
edly support the Carthaginian origin theory; the hint is there, but there
is no explicit endorsement.

On the other hand Vicente Palatino de Curzola, in his manuscript
"Tratado del derecho y justicia de la guerra que tienen los reyes de
España contra las naciones de la India occidental" of 1559 (published
in 1943), adopted the view that the Carthaginians (Phoenicians) Aristotle had mentioned were responsible for the first (or at least a) settlement. Curzola (1943:29–30) believed this because of the ruins of

buildings with unfamiliar (but probably Carthaginian) writings on them, and because the Indians told him some bearded white visitors had constructed the buildings. Apparently Curzola's (1943:30–31) real reason for claiming an earlier Carthaginian settlement was legalistic. The Carthaginian claim to the Indies had devolved upon Rome after the Third Punic War. The Pope, as heir to the Roman Emperors, had come into possession of the Indies, and he had given it to Spain. Thus Spain had a solidly based historical right to the New World.

Curzola (1943:25) did not like the Indians, whom he accused of observing neither "divine law, natural law, nor the laws of men, nor even observing the law of the ferocious beasts . . . " Therefore it was just for Spain to wage war against the Indians to return them to their rightful ruler and to make Christians of them. Sometimes the Spaniards were too zealous in their opposition to native beliefs and customs of the Indians and found it necessary to explain their conduct.

One such was Diego de Landa, who, in 1566, completed his *Relación de las cosas de Yucatán* to justify his actions toward the Indians of that province. Like so many other early works on America, it was not published in his lifetime. That first publication was an incomplete French translation in 1864. The complete version, in Spanish, appeared at Madrid in 1881. In this case the lack of publication was not critical since Landa made only two brief references to the origins of the American Indians. After relating an Indian legend of people coming from the East through twelve paths opened through the sea, Landa observed that if this were true they would be Jews (1941:16–17).

It should be noted that Landa did not offer a theory of Jewish ancestry for the Indians. He may have thought that; but, if he did, he did not express the thought. Landa did make one rather unusual observation. He disagreed with those who thought the civilization of Yucatán was imported: "These buildings have not been constructed by other nations than the Indians," he concluded (1941:18, 170–172). Landa's argument gained no great support until the nineteenth century.

Of the two dozen or so books on America which appeared between 1566 and 1572, none devoted any space specifically to the origins of the Indians. The books centered their attention primarily on the nature of the Indians—especially those by Polo de Ondegardo and Juan Matienzo. This changed in 1572 with the completion of Pedro Sarmiento de Gamboa's *Historia de los Incas*. Sarmiento's volume (first published in 1906) contained the fullest statement to date of a particular origin theory.

As a starting point, Sarmiento accepted the old Platonic legend of Atlantis. From that he postulated a pan-Atlantic continent reaching from Cadiz across the central Atlantic to include the Antilles and the American continent (1952:90). Atlantis was settled in regular order by the descendants of Noah by way of Spain and North Africa. These settlers produced a great empire which expanded even into those parts now known as Española and Cuba. When Atlantis sank beneath the sea, about 1320 B.C., the Indies, the Canaries, and Cádiz were left. Those inhabitants who remained in the westernmost parts of the old empire produced the American Indians. Sarmiento thought the presence of flood legends among the Incas reflected their memory of the drowning of Atlantis (1952:93–98).

Sarmiento felt, however, that there were certain characteristics of the Indians of Yucatán and New Spain which could not be explained by the Atlantis theory. He postulated that, after the fall of Troy, Ulysses sailed westward across the Atlantic and reached Yucatán.

> For those of that land have the Grecian bearing and Grecian dress of the nation of Ulysses. They have many Greek words and use Greek letters. I myself have seen many signs and proofs of this. They call God "Teos" which is Greek. In passing through there, I heard that these people used to preserve a ship's anchor as a venerated idol. They surely are of Greek origin . . . And from there they could have populated all those provinces of Mexico. In this way it can be seen that New Spain and its provinces were peopled by Greeks . . . and those of . . . Peru and neighboring provinces were Atlanteans (1952:98–100).

The published debate resumed in 1575 with the Augustinian friar Jerónimo Román y Zamora. Fray Jerónimo served many years in the New World before he wrote his *Repúblicas de Indias, idolatrías y gobierno en México y Perú antes de la conquista* (Salamanca, 1575). Nevertheless, he could not decide where the Indians had come from. He thought they had certainly experienced some pre-Columbian contact with Christians because some of the Yucatecan tribes knew of the cross and the Trinity, and some of those in Cholula celebrated an idolatrous version of Easter (1897:I, 58, 61, 164 ff.).

But what was their original source? Román y Zamora did not think that they descended from Hebrews. True, the Indians of Yucatán practiced circumcision in connection with religion; but that practice was not peculiar to Jews. Nor did he think word similarities such as Yucatán and Iectan (a great-great grandson of Noah) could be considered decisive, because the Indians had words that sounded like Latin, Tuscan, French, Spanish, and even Greek (1897:I, 314–321). Fray Jerónimo simply dismissed the theory that the Indians descended from ancient Spaniards as "another mistake" (1897:I, 321–322).

The only certainty, said Román y Zamora, is that the Indians "are descended from Adam." Also all men and animals except those on the Ark perished in the Flood; and those men now in the world descended from Noah's sons. But whether the line of Japheth, Shem, or Ham populated the New World or any other particular area must remain unknown, because only the Hebrews know their full genealogy (1897: I, 321–322).

Galvão's Chinese theory received a boost from a fellow-Portuguese, Pero de Magalhães, in 1576. In his *Historia de provincia Sancta Cruz, a que vulgarmente chamos Brazil* Magalhães noted the flattened face of the Brazilian Indians and suggested that they strongly resembled the Chinese (1922:II, 83). This did not constitute an endorsement of the Chinese theory, but the hint was there.

The last of the Spanish books to be considered in this section is Bernardino de Sahagún's *Historia general de las cosas de Nueva España*. Sahagún wrote it in Nahuatl between 1547 and 1569. He translated it into Spanish in the 1570's, and in that form it was used by such writers as Herrera and Torquemada at the beginning of the seventeenth century. It did not appear in published form until 1840. Sahagún's chief purpose in writing his *Historia* was to collect the vast Nahuatl folk literature before it was irreparably lost. Consequently, though he recorded the Indian origin myths at length, he paid little attention to the ultimate origin of the natives. He did, however, make a point of insisting that the Indians "are all our brothers, descendants of the stock of Adam" (1956:I, 31). Lord Kingsborough (Simon, 1836:7–8) claimed that Sahagún, whose manuscripts had at one time been confiscated, got them back with the injunction "to write nothing to prove that the Hebrews had colonized the new world." This seems hardly credible since, as will be shown in the following section of this essay, other Spaniards contemporary with Sahagún were attempting to prove a Hebrew origin for the Indians. However, it is true that Sahagún did not write that the Hebrews had colonized America.

In addition to the great number of Spanish commentators and the British and Portuguese writers already noted, one other Englishman contributed slightly to the debate on Indian origins. In 1578 William Bourne published a volume entitled *Booke Called a Treasure for Travellers*. According to Sharrow (1947:5) Bourne accepted a version of the Atlantis theory and argued that the earliest inhabitants of America were Japhethites. The great scholar of Tudor geography, E. G. R. Taylor (Bourne, 1963:xxvii), said that the *Booke* "dealt with mensuration, mathematical instruments, survey, and kindred matters." It was apparently not, as Wilmsen (1956:172) indicated, designed "to amuse leisured travellers." But Bourne's influence was negligible in the debate; none of the writers of the period before 1729 cited his work.

A summary of the course of the controversy over Indian origins in the period 1550 to 1580 reveals a rather startling condition. The most popular theory judged from the literary evidence was the Atlantean, followed closely by the Carthaginian origin theory. But a consensus of those who actually discussed the matter in the period shows a great reluctance to comment. Most of those who wrote on America did not even consider the question of the original establishment of men in the New World. Those who did comment were likely to say that a real solution did not seem possible; that the only certainty was that the Indians descended from Adam.

López de Gómara and Sarmiento and a few others supported Atlantis. Two versions of the Spanish theory were available, but no one accepted them. The Chinese, Greeks, and Carthaginians had their defenders. Sometimes, as in the case of López de Gómara and Sarmiento de Gamboa, the same writer might support two or three theories. But

Las Casas, Eden, Román y Zámora, Landa, and Sahagún all declined to commit themselves to a theory.

This reluctance to render judgment seems out of character in an age not noted for restraint in the absence of evidence.

The Ten Lost Tribes of Israel and the Ophirites

One puzzling aspect of the early thinking concerning Indian origins is the lack of any serious consideration of the possibility that the Indians descended from the Ten Lost Tribes of Israel. "This truly monkish theory . . .," this "lunatic fancy, possible only to men of a certain class, which in our time does not multiply" (Baldwin, 1871:166–167), is generally believed to have been the most obvious and thus the earliest explanation of men in America (Wauchope, 1962:3).

On the contrary, this writer was unable to locate any early explorers and historians who expressed that idea in writing. There are, however, hints scattered throughout the early literature which indicate that the opinion that the Indians were descendants of the Hebrews was current and discussed, even if no author did accept it. As early as 1511 Pedro Martir de Anglería (1944:29) left open the possibility of a Jewish origin for the natives when he reported the story that Columbus had identified Española as Ophir. Presumably, if Española were Ophir, Solomon's sailors might have left behind the progenitors of the Indians. Those who later adopted an Ophirian origin theory and expounded it invariably claimed that the New World was already populated in the time of Solomon and that his navy merely visited it. Anglería later noted (1944:308–309) in the part of his *Décadas* printed in 1530, that the Indians of Yucatán practiced circumcision, but he did not postulate a Judaic origin.

Many of the early writers have been credited with a belief in the Judaic origin of the Indians. Mrs. Simon (1836:1–26), in common with Lord Kingsborough's other disciples, claimed that virtually all the early Spanish writers believed this theory. Many modern authorities, such as Imbelloni (1956:25–26) and Wauchope (1962:53), accept the attribution of such a belief to Las Casas, Oviedo, García, Juan de Torquemada, Diego Durán, and Felipe Guamán Poma de Ayala. Of these six men, all writing before 1613, only one—Diego Durán—clearly committed himself to the Hebrew origin theory.

Juan de Torquemada was apparently the first to credit Las Casas with being a "partidario del origen hebreo." In his *Monarchia indiana* of 1613 he stated that he had found a long rationale of the theory, "in a paper where were written some phrases of the Testament of Don Frai Bartolomé de las Casas, Bishop of Chiapas; and because of this, he used in all his writings, it seems to me that it is his opinion" (1723: and because they are both in the same language and the same style that I, 24).

Yet in his *Apologética historia* Las Casas berated the "Doctor" who had postulated a Jewish origin on the basis of a few words and the practice of circumcision (1909:632–633). He also rejected the possibility of Jewish contact with America in the time of Solomon in his *Historia* (1951:I, 487–489). Furthermore, although Las Casas referred to Esdras, which was later used as the basis of the Lost Tribes theory, he did not use it in such a context (1951:II, 33–35).

The charge that Torquemada held to the Jewish theory is more readily disproved. Torquemada (1723:I, 24) continued the statement quoted above in this manner: "and if it is, I say that despite his great authority and wisdom, I am not persuaded that these Indians are of those tribes." Torquemada (1723:I, 22–27) followed this with several pages of reasons to prove, as the title of the chapter reads, "De como las Gentes de estas Indias Occidentales, no fueron Júdios, como algunos han querido sentir de ellos, y se contradicen sus razones." It is difficult to understand how anyone who even looked at Torquemada's table of contents could credit him with a belief in the Hebrew-Indian theory.

The theory that the Indians of America descended from the Hebrews, or more particularly the Ten Lost Tribes of Israel, apparently originated in published form with Joannes Fredericus Lumnius' *De Extremo Dei Iudicio et Indorum vocatione* issued at Antwerp in 1567. A second edition appeared at Venice in 1569, and the Bibliotheque nationale of Paris has a book by Lumnius called *De Vicinitate extremi judicii Dei et consummationis saeculi* (Antwerp, 1594) which it says is the "mime ouvrage que *De Extremo Dei judicio*." The book is very rare and apparently was rather obscure in its own time, for none of the Spanish authors cite it, though Solórzano (1703:11) referred to the author, and León Pinelo (1943:I, 288–290) knew of Lumnius from Solórzano. In addition Barcia included "Federico Lumnio" in the list of authors he appended to the 1729 edition of García's *Origen*.

Lumnius' *De Extremo Dei Iudicio* is largely concerned with abstruse theological points; this, together with his slim geographical knowledge, makes for a confusing book. For example, his references to India leave it unclear whether he means East or West India (1569:fol. 49v–50). References to the reasons why there were Antipodes, to Magellan, and to Americus (1569:fol. 38–39v) show that he meant the New World; yet he seems to have thought Asiatic India was not far from West India.

Lumnius introduced most of the theological arguments which were later advanced to indicate a Hebrew origin for the Indians. The basis for his story of how the Jews got to America was the fourth book of Esdras whose authority Lumnius (1569:fol. 47–47v) accepted despite its apocryphal standing. The authority of IV Kings and the prophet Isaiah supported the Esdras account (1569:fol. 46v–48v). A detailed discussion of these passages and of the development of the biblical arguments for Indian origins will be given below; briefly Lumnius' argument was that the ten tribes of Hebrews exiled to various parts of the Assyrian Empire by Shalmaneser had escaped to Arsareth which Lumnius identified as India (America).

Spanish writers who adopted or commented upon the Hebrew origin theory generally did not cite other contemporary authors as sources for their opinions. When they did, the most frequently cited work was the *Chronographia* of Gilbert Genebrard, French cosmographer and clergyman. The book appeared at Paris in 1567, and was widely used in Europe (Prince, 1915:79). But even before Genebrard broadcast the Jewish origin theory, several Spanish friars working in Mexico had arrived at the same conclusions. Two of them, Juan Suárez de Peralta and Diego Durán, had completed their manuscripts around 1580. A third, Juan de Tovar, worked with Durán and supplied both his own and Durán's work to Joseph de Acosta for use in his *Historia natural y moral* (1589–1590). Juan Suárez de Peralta's *Tratado del descubrimi-*

ento de las Indias (1580) remained unpublished until 1878. Diego Durán's *Historia de las Indias de Nueva España y Islas de Tierra Firme* (ca. 1581) appeared in 1867 and in 1880. Juan de Tovar, a relative of Durán, wrote his *Relación del origen de los indios que habitan esta Nueva España según sus historias* in the 1570's. The manuscript was lost and not found again until 1856. For many years it was referred to as the *Códice Ramírez;* only in the past two decades has Tovar been accepted as its author.

In addition to these three friars working in Mexico from Mexican materials, Miguel Cabello Valboa wrote his *Miscelánea Anthártica* at about the same time from Peruvian materials. Cabello Valboa's *Miscelánea* was first published in 1840 in a French-language excerpt. A copy of the manuscript was edited and published in 1945. The *Miscelánea* proposed a non-Jewish Ophirian origin for the Indians, and will be used here to clarify the distinctions between Jewish and Ophirian theories so frequently ignored in modern studies (Imbelloni, 1956: 37–45).

Although Suárez de Peralta, Durán, and Cabello Valboa remained unpublished until the nineteenth century, a discussion of their works is useful to illustrate the growing complexity of the discussion and to point up the developments of and differences between the Jewish, Canaanite, and Ophirian origin theories. All three books circulated in manuscript and did therefore contribute to the expansion of the controversy, even though they were not widely available.

Juan Suárez de Peralta was the earliest identifiable Spaniard to endorse the Lost Tribes of Israel theory, and even his acceptance was qualified. He based his opinion "in the authority of Chapter xiii of the fourth book of *Esdras*" (1949:1–2). The passages to which Suárez de Peralta referred read:

These are the ten tribes which were led away captive out of their own land in the days of Josiah the king, which (tribes) Shalmanassar the king of the Assyrians led away captive; he carried them across the river; and (thus) they were transported into another land. But they took council among themselves, that they would leave the multitude of the heathen, and go forth into a land further distant, where the human race had never dwelt, there at least to keep their statutes which they had not kept in their own land. And they entered by the narrow passages of the river Euphrates. For the Most High then wrought wonders for them and stayed the springs of the River until they were passed over. And through that country there was a great way to go, (a journey) of a year and a half; and that region was called Arzareth. There they have dwelt until the last times; and now when they are about to come again, the Most High will again stay the springs of the River, that they may be able to pass over (IV Esdras 13:40–47).

Suárez de Peralta interpreted this to mean that the Ten Tribes taken captive by Shalmaneser had escaped to a land called Arsareth. This Arsareth was obviously near America and some of the Jews had migrated to it. He supported this conclusion by citing (1949:2–5) the similarity of certain Aztec words to Hebrew words, and by claiming both peoples had similar idolatries. He did not, however, claim the Lost Tribes as the exclusive populators of the New World. In fact, he thought that the first settlers probably came before the Flood. His authority for this belief was Genesis 6:4, which said that there were "giants on the Earth" in the days before the Flood. Since bones of giants had been reported in Mexico and Peru, obviously America had been peopled by giants who had drowned in the Flood (1949:7).

Suárez de Peralta found it difficult to believe that all the Indians descended from the same people or from the same colony. He did not think that the natives of Labrador and Florida came from the same stock as those near the Strait of Magellan. Consequently, he accepted the Carthaginian theory (1949:5) to explain the population of the Islands. He further proposed an Ethiopian or Egyptian origin for certain Indians of New Spain because they shared with the Egyptians and Ethiopians the custom of allowing women to enter business and public affairs, and "the men stay at home to weave and labor; and the women urinate standing and the men while seated," and both men and women carry out the necessities of nature in public (1949:5).

Suárez de Peralta also introduced (1949:6–7) the question whether the Indians descended from Canaan, the son of Ham cursed by Noah for his father's sin. His opinion on this point was somewhat unclear. Since the Indies were peopled from various sources, the opinion that they descended from "the accursed Canaan, can thus be true in part and not in whole." But the descendants of Ham (Canaan) were widely dispersed and all the people who came to America were either his descendants or were influenced by them, for "realmente los indios proceden del maldito Chanaan" (1949:7).

The Canaanite theory of Indian origins (or as it is frequently called by those who confuse the object of the curse, the theory that the Indians descended from Ham) was not a *Jewish* origin theory. To qualify as of Jewish origin the progenitors must be members of one of the twelve tribes of Hebrews. The designation of all Hebrews as Jews, though technically incorrect, is an ancient device. Most of the Hebrew tribes disappeared after the "captivity" and those left were predominantly of the tribe of Judah. The custom grew of calling all Hebrews Jews. Israel was the generic designation of all the tribes of Hebrews.

The Canaanites were not Hebrews, even under the loosest interpretations. The modern tendency to think of most peoples mentioned in the Old Testament as Jews confuses the issue. Suárez evidently did not distinguish these peoples very clearly. Nonetheless, the Canaanite origin theory is a separate tradition in itself as later writers would indicate with greater clarity. No doubt it was current throughout the sixteenth century. It seems unlikely that those who supported Indian slavery would have ignored the "curse of Ham/Canaan." It does appear, however, that Suárez de Peralta first expressed it.

Diego Durán was much less equivocal in his theorizing. Since, he said, he had not received a revelation from God, which was the only way to determine for certain where the Indians originated, he would resort to conjecture. He concluded that the Indians must be descended from Jews. His opinion was based on the strange ways and customs and the lowly conversation of the natives; their "way of life, ceremonies, rites, and superstitions, omens, and hypocrisies;" all so like the Jews' that the Indians themselves must be Jews (1951:I, 1).

Durán found support for his belief in observations of Indian cultures which, he thought, matched very well with the biblical descriptions of the Jews. Unlike Suárez de Peralta who used the apocryphal Esdras IV on which to base his theory, Durán relied on the Bible itself. His source was the second book of Kings (RSV, 17:6, 18): "In the ninth year of Hoshea the king of Assyria captured Samaria, and he carried the Israelites away to Assyria . . . Therefore the Lord was very angry with Israel, and removed them out of his sight; none was left but the tribe of Judah only."

Durán's version was somewhat garbled by the use of the abbreviation "etc." to refer to what happened to the Israelites after their arrival in Assyria. Apparently he referred to the Arsareth legend from Esdras. As a consequence, his description of the remote land [Arsareth] seems to be a reference to Assyria (1949:I, 2). Evidently the story was so well known that it did not require elaboration.

Durán found additional confirmation in the story of Hosea (Hosea 1:10) that God had promised to multiply the people of Israel like the sands of the sea. Surely, he argued, this promise was fulfilled by the multitudes the Spanish found in the New World (1951:I, 2–3). Furthermore, he noted, the Indians (of Mexico) had traditions of long journeys, such as the one from Assyria to Arsareth. They also had traditions of flights, such as the exodus from Egypt. Other "proofs" included common traditions of earthquakes which swallowed evil men and of objects (manna) falling from heaven; and the fact that an old Indian had begun his tale of the origins of his people with the words "In the beginning God created the heavens and the Earth." This story, Durán reported, roughly paralleled Genesis 1–2, 6, and 11. Finally Durán compared the secret mountain sacrifices, legends of pests, plagues, wars, and other disasters, child sacrifice, and cannibalism. He thought all these legends and myths were common to both the Indians and the Lost Tribes of Israel.

At this point Durán introduced his strongest argument: ". . . that which most forces me to believe that these Indians are of Hebrew lineage is the strange pertinacity they have in not casting away their idolatries and superstitions, living by them as did their ancestors, as David said in the 105th [106th] Psalm" (1951:I, 8). The relevant passages read:

> They served their idols,
>   which became a snare to them.
> They sacrificed their sons
>   and their daughters to the demons;
> They poured out innocent blood,
>   the blood of their sons and daughters,

whom they sacrificed to the idols of Canaan;
and the land was polluted with blood.
(Ps. 106:36–38)

The friars of Mexico, working as they did with the Aztec legends of vast migrations, came more readily to the Lost Tribes theory than those working in other areas. The legendary wanderings of the Aztecs found a responsive chord in the Christian steeped in the traditions of the Jewish Exodus. By the last quarter of the sixteenth century the work of such men as Motolinía, Sahagún, Durán, Tovar, and Suárez de Peralta had made the Aztecs' oral history available. It was not until the Aztecs' own views about their history became widely known that the obvious, though superficial, parallels with Jewish traditions could be made. Furthermore, it was not until these comparisons had been made that writers began to make extensive use of biblical and related traditions to explain and support their theories. Most writers on Indian origins before 1580 did not use the Bible in constructing their theories. Many relied exclusively on nonbiblical literary sources. Most went no further into the Scripture than to insist that all men descended from Adam through Noah. It will be noted that the basis for the Lost Tribes theory lies primarily in the Apocrypha, not in the Bible. The Apocrypha were widely known to the educated classes of Europe through the numerous commentaries on the Bible. It is uncertain how much of this knowledge filtered down to the commoners.

Once begun, the practice of basing origin theories in Scripture mushroomed. But at no time was this method used to the exclusion of others. Biblical exegesis was useless without information about the Indians usable for comparative purposes. Nor did biblical exegesis ever dominate the search for known quantities with which to compare the Indians. At any given time there were probably more men working from nonscriptural sources for their comparative material.

Just as those more familiar with New Spain than with Peru tended to accept some form of the Lost Tribe theory, those who were most familiar with Peru tended toward the Ophirian theory. Some confusion over what the Ophirian theory is has resulted from the fact that those who first mentioned the story did not make clear what they meant

(Anglería, 1944:29; Las Casas, 1951:I, 487–489). Did they mean to say that the Indians descended from people who went to Ophir in the time of Solomon? In that case the Indians would be Jews. Some writers have taken this as the meaning without realizing that there was an alternative (Imbelloni, 1956:37–45). It seems most likely that the writers who referred to Ophir meant to show that in the time of Solomon the land of Ophir was already settled and named. The settlement came long before Solomon, and it was a non-Jewish people who settled it.

The passages relating to Ophir are I Kings 9:26–28; 10:11; and II Chronicles 8:18; 9:10 (RSV):

King Solomon built a fleet of ships at Ezion-geber, which is near Eloth on the shore of the Red Sea, in the land of Edom. And Hiram sent with the fleet his servants, seamen who were familiar with the sea, together with the servants of Solomon; and they went to Ophir, and brought from there gold, to the amount of four hundred and twenty talents; and they brought it to King Solomon.

Moreover the fleet of Hiram, which brought gold from Ophir, brought from Ophir a great amount of almug wood and precious stones (I Kings 9:26–28, 10:11).

This story is repeated almost verbatim in II Chron. 8:18, 9:10—the only difference being that "almug wood" is "algum wood" in the Chronicles version. Most writers of the period included II Chron. 9:21 ("For the king's ships went to Tarshish with the servants of Hirum; once every three years the ships of Tarshish used to come bringing gold, silver, ivory, apes, and peacocks.") as part of the Ophir story, although they understood that the voyage lasted three years (Acosta, 1940:40–43).

The first clear statement of the Ophirian theory, which traced the Indians to a great-great-great grandson of Noah named Ophir, appeared about 1572 in the *apparatus criticus* written for the famous Polyglot Bible of Antwerp (1569–1572) by the editor, Benito Arias Montano, chaplain to Philip II (Bell, 1922:19–38; Rivet, 1960:25). The comments on the Ophirian origin of the Indians occur in the portion of the *apparatus* dealing with Genesis 10:25 ("And unto Eber

were born two sons; the name of one was Peleg; for in his days was
the earth divided; and his brother's name was Joktan.") Arias Montano called this section "Phaleg, sive de gentium sedibus primis, orbisque terræ situ," and, as a consequence, writers who knew of his
arguments referred to his *Phaleg* (Acosta, 1962:LXVII; Córdova
Salinas, 1958:1163).

One of the men who read Arias Montano's *Phaleg* had already
worked out a similar thesis independently. Miguel Cabello Valboa
completed his *Miscelánea Anthártica* around 1582. After reading
Phaleg and discovering that its author agreed with him, he arranged
his *Miscelánea* for publication. He completed the reorganization of his
materials about 1586, but was not able to publish it. A French translation of a small part of the manuscript appeared in 1840, and a copy of
the manuscript was published at Quito in 1945 and at Lima in 1951
with notes on the original* (Cabello Valboa, 1951:7). So far as this
writer was able to determine, the *Miscelánea* was the first book devoted
primarily to the question of the origins of the American Indians
(Lumnius devoted only a dozen pages to the question), but García's
Origen was the first published book exclusively on the subject.

Cabello Valboa set a very difficult task for himself; indeed it was an
impossible one. He planned to trace "the origin of these Indian nations
from the beginning of the world" (1951:3). This necessitated discovering when the first settlers came to America, how they got there,
from which part of the Old World they departed for the New World,
and by which genealogy they were connected to recognized biblical
lines. Actually he proposed to write what must amount to little less
than a history of human migrations. His sources of information consisted of the Bible, the commentators on the Bible, related texts, such
as the Apocrypha, ancient authors, modern comments on America; and
his own experience as a missionary in South America. His method was
exegetical and comparative.

The author solved his greatest problem by deciding, on the basis of
the similarities of the names *Peru* and *Ophir*, that the Indians descended from Ophir. Another proof lay in the similarity of the name
Yucatán with *Iectan*, the name of Ophir's father (1951:4–5). Cabello

* See the discussion of Cubero Sebastian, 1684, below in Chapter III, p. 83.

Valboa now knew where to start his search for the way the Indians got to America. He had first to determine when Ophir and Iectan or their descendants left Mesopotamia. That proved easy. Given the diversity of languages in America, they must have left after Babel. After the confusion of tongues, Ophir moved to the Far East where he became the ancestor of the seafaring peoples of that area (1951:73–77). From there the descendants of Ophir went to America where they settled in Peru and New Spain.

Cabello Valboa again supported his contention by pointing up the derivation of *Peru* from *Ophir,* Peru having been named in honor of the racial ancestor of the natives (1951:93–96; 159–166; 189–191). In addition, he said, the story of the voyage to Ophir in Solomon's day utilized the word "Parbaim," meaning "the two Perus." The second "Peru" was Yucatán, named in honor of Ophir's father (1951:110). To those who argued that the word "Peru" was not current in that country when the Spanish arrived, Cabello Valboa responded that such was true. The natives had forgotten the name. However, it was pre-served in the names of geographical features where the Spaniards found it and revived it (1951:108–109).

Cabello Valboa did not rely wholly on biblical allusions. He spent several pages comparing the Indians of America with those of the East Indies. He argued (1951:195–200) that both used cotton for cloth-ing and that their clothing styles were similar. Furthermore, both sat on the ground rather than use chairs or benches, and neither used ta-bles. But what of the difference in skin color of the Indians and their progenitors? Skin color, he said, changed because of "the influence of the Sky, and the force of the Stars, and the aridity of the winds which over a long period of time, turned the whiteness of their faces into that more or less black color" (1951:54, 226).

From time to time Cabello Valboa interrupted his elaboration of his own story to take issue with a rival theory. He disagreed with Alejo Vanegas and the Carthaginian theory because in his opinion Hanno went to the Canaries and thence to the Red Sea. He did not go to the Indies. Cabello Valboa argued that Carthaginian cultural traits, reli-gion, and writing were absent from the New World; therefore, the Carthaginians surely had not come to America (1951:96–104).

The Indians did not descend from the Hebrews either, Cabello declared. He referred to a lecture by one Juan de el Caño at Salamanca in 1580 which traced the Indians to a Jewish ancestry on the basis of word comparisons. Cabello thought language comparison an improper and useless tool in tracing origins. There were too many languages in America for such a method to prove valid. He maintained that in some places the man and woman of the same family spoke different languages, and it was dishonest for a woman to speak a man's language, and shameful for a man to speak a woman's. Anyway, he concluded, the Jews had an alphabet; the Indians did not (1951:104–105).

To take a specific example, he continued, consider the Quechua language. It indeed had some words similar to Hebrew, but it also had some words similar to French or Spanish, though they had different meanings. "Mayo" in Spanish referred to the fifth month of the year; in Quechua it meant "river." "Macho" in Spanish applied to the virile sex; but in Quechua it mean "old" (1951:105–106). Therefore, Cabello Valboa rejected the Judaic origin as untenable.

Cabello Valboa was not entirely correct in his refutation of Vanegas. Florián de Ocampo used the Hanno story; Vanegas did not. He relied on Aristotle's Carthaginian story which was independent of the Hanno tradition.

The *Miscelánea* appears to be little more than a collection of several papers Cabello Valboa prepared at different times on the subject of Ophir in the Indies. His reorganization for publication was not wholly successful. The book is filled with long digressions and virtually incomprehensible exegetical ramblings. The arguments are generally consistent, but continuity is frequently lost.

Since both Las Casas and Cabello Valboa derived the Indians from the East Indies, why did they differ so much? Las Casas, though he did propose an East Indian origin in his *Apologética historia,* never firmly committed himself to any origin theory. He specifically denied that Solomon visited the New World; that point, however, was incidental to Cabello Valboa's argument. Las Casas, and those who later postulated an East Indian origin, differed from the Ophirites in a very basic fashion. True, both groups brought the Indians from the same place. But those who held to the Ophirian theory were not content to settle for a geographic derivation: they had to trace the *East* Indians to *their* origins. The Ophirian and Lost Tribes origin theories differed from most other theories in that they traced the Americans to their ultimate origin by connecting them with the biblical genealogies.

The analysis of these unpublished, but not unused, works of the 1580's illustrates the growing complexities and subtleties of the controversy over the origins of the American Indians. From the simple propositions of Oviedo in 1535, and the relatively uncomplicated solutions of mid-century, the "debate" developed into the largely theological exegetics of Suárez de Peralta and Durán, and the occultism of Cabello Valboa.

El Primer nueva corónica y buen gobierno by Phelipe Guamán Poma de Ayala (written between 1587 and 1613 and published for the first time in 1936) was an even more esoteric production. Poma de Ayala was "of pure Indian blood," and his language is only vaguely Spanish. His orthography is generally identifiable, but the syntax and style lend his writing a large measure of obscurity (Means, 1923). The most recent edition contains the original text and an "interpretation" for modern Spanish readers, which amounts to a translation.

This modern translation is frequently inaccurate. For example, Poma de Ayala wrote that ". . . se escrive q. sera desde la fundacion del mundo dos millon y seycientos y doze anos desde el comienso hasta el acabo"; which clearly means that 2,000,612 years will pass between the beginning and the end of the world. Yet the translator renders it "desde la creación del mundo hasta la actualidad han transcurrido 2'000,612 [sic] anos" (1956:285, 13). Sometimes the translator inserted entire passages not in the original. Poma de Ayala (1956:307) writes that "desta generacion comensaron a multiplicar y la descendencia y multiplico despues a estos les llamaron dioses y lo tubieron aci." The translation reads:

Los hombres de esta generación comenzaron a aumentar rápidamente, llegando a ser muy numerosas sus descendientes, guardando siempre veneración a sus antecesores a los que llamaban sus Dioses y adorándolos como tales por más de seis mil seiscientos trece anos de los cuales de puede descontar para major exactitud los ocho cientos anos que corresponden a la época en que se enseñorearon y habitaron en este reino (1956:35).

Apparently those who hold to the belief that all civilization began in America (at Tihuanacu) are using Poma de Ayala for their own purposes. The chief contention of that school requires considerable antiquity for man in America (Posnansky, 1945:I, 5). The late Arthur Posnansky, the long-time leader of this group, edited Poma's book in 1944, and the "interpreter" of the last edition, Luís Bustos Gálvez, incorporated many of Posnansky's notes into the text. The result generally is to indicate the great antiquity needed by the Posnansky school. Bustos Gálvez also makes Poma say (1956:35, 13) that "the first white men in the world" were in Peru. It is easy to do such things to Poma's text. The syntax is so obscure that meaning cannot always be derived. Furthermore, Poma does appear to accept a greater antiquity for man in the New World than most other commentators of his day.

Poma wrote of one of Noah's sons coming "god-brought" to the Indies (1956:293), and he attributed orderly, civilized life to the Incas around the time of David (1956:294). It seems as if he thought men came to America shortly after the Flood and developed independently there. The bulk of his book concerned what was happening in America at the time of important events in the Old World.

Juan de Castellanos (1955:II, 91–92), in his *Elegías de varones ilustres de Indias* of 1589, wrote of the reaction of Columbus' men when they first encountered Indians:

> Si son sátiros estos, o silvanos,
> Y ellas aquellas ninfas de Aristeo:
> O son faunos, lascivos y lozanos,
> O las nereides, hijas de Nereo,
> O driades que llaman, o nayades,
> De quien trataban las antiquedades . . .
>
> Pues no son en estado de inocencia
> Que hijos son de Adán y descendientes.

These thoughts, placed in the minds of the first Europeans to see the Indians, tell much more about the poet's own time than about 1492. Columbus' men thought they were in Asia and would have no reason to wonder about the humanity of the men they found there. But in Castellanos' own time the ferment over the origin and nature of the Indians was so great that it was even being read into the past where it did not belong. It is indicative of the confusion over the questions concerning the Indians that, although Castellanos put many questions into the minds of his characters, the only answer he gave was that the Indians were, after all, the sons of Adam.

That alone was certain.

CHAPTER II

Acosta and García, 1589-1607

Joseph de Acosta and the Acostan Tradition

EUROPEANS MADE surprisingly little headway before 1589 in their attempts to discover the origins of the American Indians. The usual method for tracing origins consisted of noting certain cultural affinities—dress, speech, manner, religion—between the Americans and some Old World people of antiquity, and then inventing a mode of transporting that people to America. Infrequently the comparisons might be made with contemporary peoples to the extent of noting and explaining the differences which had developed since the settlement of the New World. On the whole, the writers presumed a large measure of cultural stability; that is, implicit in their works was the belief that cultures of antiquity had not changed much in the intervening millennia.

Joseph de Acosta changed that pattern. Acosta went to Peru as a Jesuit missionary in 1570. He achieved sufficient importance to be included in Viceroy Toledo's train in his trip through Charcas and in his war against the Chiriguanos of the Chaco (Acosta, 1940:iv). He probably knew Pedro Sarmiento de Gamboa, Toledo's "Admiral." Acosta spent seventeen years in the Indies—most of them in Peru. In 1586 he went to Mexico where he met Juan de Tovar and made extensive notes on Tovar's history of the Mexican Indians. The following year he returned to Spain (1940:xiii–xix).

Acosta began to write his own history of the New World around 1580, and completed the first two books by 1584. On his return to Spain he set about preparing them for publication. In 1589 they were published in Latin at Salamanca. Acosta then translated them into Spanish and published them as the first quarter of his great *Historia natural y moral de las Indias* (Sevilla, 1590). A second edition followed in 1591, and a third in 1608. Edward Grimston's English translation appeared in 1604.

Joseph de Acosta, writing almost a hundred years after Columbus' discovery, was the first to approach the problems involved in getting the Indians to America, and tracing their origins, in a truly objective fashion. Acosta maintained that experience was more reliable than philosophy, and that it could reveal more than any "reason or philosophic demonstration." It was lack of experience which led the ancients to deny the existence of the Antipodes. Modern experience had proved that there were Antipodes, that they could be reached, and that the Tropics were habitable (1940:15, 29–44, 93).

Since experience had proved men did indeed live in America; and since all men must have descended from Adam, they must of necessity have come from Europe, Africa, or Asia. Rather than jump into cultural comparisons to find the Old World counterpart of the Indians, Acosta decided that he should first examine the situation of America with respect to the Old World, both geographically and historically, to discover how men *could* have got to the New World. Only then could he determine which *men* had actually come (1940:61). Acosta had already expressed his disdain for those who argued that the name "Peru" derived from "Ophir," or "Yucatán" from "Yectan"; or the Inca names "Tito" or "Paulo" from "Titus" or "Paul." Word comparisons, he maintained, were "too weak as arguments to sustain such grand conclusions" (1940:52).

How could the first men have come to America? It seemed unlikely to Acosta that there was a second Ark to carry them, nor could he credit an angel with that work (1940:61). Furthermore, he said,

I am not convinced that the first Indians came to this New World as a result of purposeful navigation, nor do I wish to concede that the ancients had developed the art of navigation whereby men of this day pass from place to place on the Ocean with certainty, nor do I find evidence of so notable a voyage in all antiquity (1940:63).

So far as Acosta could determine, the ancients had no lodestone or compass, and could not, therefore, have made the voyage across the Atlantic (1940:63).

What of accidental discovery by being blown off course and to the Indies? "It seems to me quite likely that in times past men came to the Indies driven unwillingly by the wind," Acosta (1940:72) answered; but he did not think this an adequate explanation of the American population:

The reason which forces me to say that the first men of these Indies came from Europe or Asia is so as not to contradict the Holy Scripture which clearly teaches that all men descended from Adam, and thus we can give no other origin to man in the Indies (1940:75–76).

By the same token the beasts of the New World as well as its men must be derived from the Old World; for does not the Bible say that only those in the Ark were saved? Was it reasonable to think the settlers who came to America either intentionally or because of storm, though they might have women with them, would also have wolves, tigers, and other ravenous beasts on the ship? "It was more than enough for men to escape with their lives, driven against their will by the tempest without carrying foxes and wolves and feeding them at sea" (1940:76).

Since the beasts could not have swum the broad ocean, and since they probably did not come in ships with men (not even for sport), and since a separate ark or angelic aid were implausible, how did they get to America? And would not a passage usable by beasts be usable by man also? Acosta was forced by these considerations to conjecture "that the new world we call the Indies is not completely divided and separated from the other World," and in the undiscovered North, or South, the two worlds had a land connection. At worst, he concluded, they were separated by only a narrow strait, such as that of Magellan, which could be crossed by man and beast easily (1940:77–81).

Acosta now had his ground rules, but he still did not have his Indians. Before giving his own opinion, he commented on those theories he had already heard. He contemptuously dismissed the Atlantis origin theory saying that "only children and old women" could believe what Plato wrote of that island (1940:84). Acosta was equally disdainful of the supposed Jewish origin of the Indians. True, both Indians and Jews were "fearful, submissive, ceremonious . . . and deceitful," but the Hebrews possessed writing and the Indians did not. The Hebrews also loved silver, but the Indians did not. The Hebrews practiced circumcision; but Acosta knew of no Indians who did. (He did not credit the reports from Yucatán.) Furthermore, the Jews jealously preserved their heritage wherever they went and Esdras specifically stated they went to Arsareth to keep their laws. But, if the Indians were Jewish they had forgotten their lineage, their law, their ceremonies, their messiahs, and their entire Judaism (1940:87–88).

It was difficult to discover the origins of the Americans because they had no written traditions. Acosta thought, however, that the Indians came to the New World little by little and that they came by land or across a narrow strait. The major cause of their coming was the nearness of the continents in some undiscovered area. The first to have come a few thousand years ago would have been savage hunters driven by hunger or loss of homeland or overpopulation. These people settled down and retained little of their former culture. They developed their own civil institutions which were not beastly or "sin razón," but worthy of respect (1940:89–90, 447–448). That was as far as Acosta could go, for it would be "rash and presumptuous" to attempt to determine the precise origins of the Indians (1940:90).

Acosta returned to the matter of Indian origins from time to time in the remainder of his *Historia*. He spoke (1940:92) of freeing the Indians from the belief that they had originated in the New World. Later, the question of corn arose: "Whence came *maíz* to the Indies and why this grain is called Turkish grain in Italy is sooner asked than answered. Actually I found no evidence of this grain in antiquity" (1940:267). God evidently gave each area of the world what it needed: wheat to the Old World; corn to the New. Also, either the plants somehow survived the Flood or God made them anew afterward. They did not have to migrate. Acosta also returned to the problem of animals in the New World to explain the beasts peculiar to America—llama, vicuña, alpaca, et al. Acosta did not think this fact greatly important; America was not the only section of the world with a unique fauna (1940:321–326).

Acosta's arguments had a far-reaching importance. He was the first writer to attempt a careful analysis of the conditions which must be met before *any* origin for the Indians could be determined. He was not the first to postulate a land bridge connecting the two worlds; that was integral to Sarmiento de Gamboa's Atlantis theory. But he was the first to propose a land connection—or near connection—which did not derive from some European legend. Acosta thought such a thing necessary to explain how such masses of animals and men could get to America. Sarmiento utilized a disappearing land bridge which was itself the homeland of the Indians and whose inundation hid the Indians from Europe. Acosta postulated a continuing "connection" which induced men to come to America because it was there. The geographical remoteness of the bridge and the low cultural level of the migrants were responsible for Europe's lack of knowledge of the New World.

Acosta implied that America was settled as a natural consequence of its existence and the gradual expansion of primitive peoples. The only areas where such a connection could exist lay in the far south or the far north. Tierra del Fuego might connect with the East Indies by a southern continent. In the north, Greenland might connect with America; or northeast Asia and America might be joined in the region of Anian, a kingdom and strait presumed to lie in the Alaska-Siberia region.

Acosta's arguments constitute a denial of the utility of sixteenth century methodology. If, as he claimed (1940:89–90), the first inhabitants were primitive hunters who settled in America, became an agricultural people, and then developed their *own* civil customs, then it would be impossible to trace the original Indians by the traditional method of comparing cultural traits. The cultural characteristics present in modern Indian civilizations would not be the ones they brought with them. Similarities between Old and New World peoples and civilizations would not be indicative of origin. Presumably the Indian cultures could be influenced by later arrivals. Even Acosta admitted the probability that the migration into America continued over a long period, and that there may have been some trans-Atlantic contact (1940: 89, 72).

The question of the origins of the Indians had long since ceased to have any substantial practical importance. The enslavement of the Indians and their forced labor, long permitted in practice, was now argued almost entirely on the legal and religious level. The judicial activities of Viceroy Toledo in the 1570's and the legal briefs of Polo de Ondegardo (1571) and Juan Matienzo (ca. 1573) were concerned with the legal and religious circumstances under which an Indian could be forced to work. The nature of the Indians, or whether they descended from Atlantis, the Ten Lost Tribes of Israel, Solomon's sailors, or shipwrecked Europeans had become an intriguing intellectual problem—a matter of curiosity—but of no great importance. Only on a few occasions in the future would the questions of Indian origins become of vital importance; and then only to certain peculiar racial, religious or occult groups.

Acosta's great attempt to establish "ground rules" for an intellectual dispute was of lasting importance. Few writers after 1590 were unaware of his *Historia natural y moral de las Indias*. Some ignored it and its arguments, and some tried to refute it. The logical completeness of his argument was itself a limitation. The question of Indian origins *was* an intriguing one. Acosta, in arguing that the old approaches were invalid, could not discover any new criteria by which the subject could be studied. Unless or until such new criteria were found, the cultural "autocthony" aspect of Acosta's argument must be accepted—in which case the debate must be discontinued—or rejected in favor of continuing the old investigative procedures.

The continued employment of the cultural comparison technique indicates a general rejection of the cultural independence of the American aborigines and a continuing inability to find—or even to seek eagerly—new ways of investigating such problems. This should not cause surprise. The application of archæology to the study of ancient peoples had not begun. Archæology was not used in America until the late eighteenth century. Furthermore, the union of archæology with comparative anatomy and ethnology to produce a scientific study of early man did not come about until the nineteenth century. For the most part the men of the sixteenth, seventeenth, and eighteenth centuries conceived the problem of human diffusion in geographical, historical, ethnological, and theological terms. The age did not recognize that the problem of Indian origins might have two distinct aspects. The idea that the Indians might have different biological and cultural derivations was inherent in Acosta's concept of cultural independence for the Indians. But he did not develop significantly the idea of independence. The possibility of separate tribal and cultural origins would have had little meaning to the men of the sixteenth or seventeenth century. Their theology did not allow enough time or diversity for such an idea.

The seventeen years between Acosta's *Historia natural y moral de las Indias* and the publication of Gregorio García's *Origen de los indios* in 1607 was marked by the appearance of an enormous amount of material on the New World. Most writers did not discuss the origin of the natives of America, but their testimony about the customs and nature of the Indians was widely used by those who were interested in the question. Many of the more important descriptive works were available only in manuscript. Martín de Morúa's *Origen de los reyes del gran Reino del·Perú* (1590) was published in 1911; the same author's *Relación geográfico-estadística del Perú* (1577–1600) appeared first in 1925. The *Historia eclesiástica indiana* (1596) of the Franciscan Gerónimo de Mendieta was not published until 1870, but it was used extensively by Juan de Torquemada in the early seventeenth century. Reginaldo de Lizárraga's *Descripción de las Indias* (ca. 1602), published in 1907, also added to the growing literature on the Indies.

Published works which greatly increased knowledge of America and contributed indirectly to the expansion of interest in the origin question appeared frequently. Giovanni Botero's four volume *L'relatione universali* (Rome, 1591) went through Italian editions of 1591, 1592–1593, 1596, and 1599. A Spanish translation came out in 1599; Latin versions appeared in 1596 and 1598; and English editions were published in 1601, 1611, and 1630. The material on America filled folios 134 through 182 of Part I in the Valladolid edition of 1599. This part was not included in the two Latin editions. Considerable information was also provided by Bernardo de Vargas Machuca in his two anti-Las Casas books: *Apologías y discursos de las conquistas occidentales* (1595) and the *Milicia y descripción de las Indias* (Madrid, 1599). Both commented extensively on the Indians; Vargas Machuca (1892:II, 76–99) was almost wholly unfavorable toward the Las Casas school of thought about the nature of the Indians.

In addition to English translations of Botero, Acosta (1604) and Anglería (1607), the English readers interested in America had the massive compilation of *The Principal Navigations Voyages Traffiques & Discoveries of the English Nation* by Richard Hakluyt, published first in 1589 and in revised form in 1598–1600. French readers had various editions of translations of Spanish works. They also had the fantastic accounts of André Thevet's *La cosmographie universelle* (Paris, 1575) and *Les singularities de la France antarctique* (Paris, ca. 1557), and Jean de Lery's *Histoire d'un voyage fait en la terre du Bresil* (La Rochelle, 1578).

Both published and unpublished materials from this period evidenced a continued and growing disillusionment with classical authority. One of the bitterest criticisms was Peter Albinus' pamphlet, *A Treatise on Foreign Languages and Unknown Islands,* which appeared near the end of the sixteenth century in Latin. Albinus (1884:56–57) denounced the ancients: "What, pray can be found more ridiculous than such men? What, in the name of heaven, moved them, when they had explored almost no portion of the world in which they were placed, to dream that there were other worlds where they could not penetrate?" After pondering that for a few passages, Albinus concluded that "Experience, the mistress of everything, has refuted the false assertions of all of them" (1884:56–57).

Spaniards too, not usually thought to be in tune with the developing rationalism of the late sixteenth and early seventeenth centuries, pondered the errors of the ancients. Indeed, they had been curious about those errors for generations. Generally speaking, Spaniards were not so critical as Albinus. Acosta was doubtless atypical. The most prevalent critique was exemplified by the *Primera parte de los problemas y secretos maravillosos de las Indias* published by the Mexican *médico* Juan de Cárdenas, in 1591.

Cárdenas was not content to say the ancients had erred; he wanted to know why they had erred. The ancients had thought the Burning Zone uninhabitable, and in strictest philosophy it should be. Why were the Tropics habitable? Cárdenas found the answer in the cooling effect of the great variety of altitudes, the summer rains, and the equal lengths of the days and nights (1913:20–23, 45–48). Although the Tropics (and America) were habitable, Cárdenas thought the honor of the ancients was partly saved by virtue of the fact that the climate of the Indies had a degenerative effect on man; that people born in the New World did not live as long as Europeans; and that even Spaniards born in the Indies were more delicate than those born in Spain (1913: 154–163).

The influence of Joseph de Acosta on the literature of Indian origins in the period 1590–1607 was apparent, though the literature retained much of its pre-Acosta flavor. The Carthaginian theory received some support in Agustín Dávila Padilla's *Historia de la fundación y discurso de la Provincia de Santiago de México, de la Orden de Predicadores* (Madrid, 1596). Dávila made a brief comparison of Carthaginian and Indian sacrificial practices, but he did not commit himself to the theory (1955:77–79). Antonio de Herrera y Tordesillas, writing around 1600 in his *Historia general de los hechos de los castellanos en las Islas y Tierra Firme del Mar Océano* (completed and published in 1613; "Part I" issued at Madrid in 1601), also referred to Aristotle's version of the Carthaginian legend. Herrera pointed out (1934–1957:II, 11–13) that Aristotle said the island was found and left uninhabited. The Carthaginian tale as given by Florián de Ocampo, who included the Hanno tradition, found full support in Father Lizárraga's *Descripción* (1946:19).

The Atlantis possibility received little comment. Lizárraga (1946: 19), Herrera (1934–1957:II, 11–13), and Enrico Martín, in his *Reportorio* of 1606 (1606:103–104), all rejected it as untenable. The other writers ignored it. This theory, the most frequently accepted possibility before 1580, seemed to have lost most of its support by 1600.

Similarly, no version of the Ophirian story got any support. The Jesuit Anello Oliva, in his *Historia del Reino y Provincias del Perú* (written 1598; published Lima, 1895), quoted Acosta to the effect that the name "Peru" was derived from the name of a river (1895:4–5). Herrera also referred to the supposed derivation of "Peru" from "Ophir" but rejected this argument (1934–1957:II, 13–14).

Two writers of the period, Mendieta and Hakluyt, contributed new theories of Indian origins. Two others, Herrera and Enrico Martín, offered theories based largely in Acosta's arguments. Mendieta, who worked in Mexico, wrote only briefly about the origins of the Indians. He referred to the practice of circumcision among certain Indians of Mexico, but he did not commit himself to a Jewish connection (1870: 107–108). Actually, he attributed the theories he did explain to other men. To Father Olmos he attributed the opinion that the Indians came from one of three places at one of three times: from Babylonia when the division of tongues occurred; or later from the land of "Sichen" in the time of Jacob, when some fled that land; or when the Israelites displaced the Canaanites, Amorites, and Jebusites. To some unspecified "others" he attributed theories of Indian origins based on the stories of the captivity and dispersion of the Jews, and in the flight of the Jews when Rome destroyed Jerusalem in the time of Vespasian. But, as for himself, "because there is no reason or foundation for any of these opinions which could affirm one more than the other, it is better to leave it undecided and let each take the one which best suits him" (1870:145).

Hakluyt's contribution to the origin literature consisted of publishing a section from a manuscript by the Welshman David Powell relating to the pre-Columbian discovery of America by the Welsh Prince Madoc (ca. 1170). Hakluyt thought the story a true one. In brief, it told of the flight of Madoc to escape the civil wars of Wales. He and his followers sailed to the west where they settled, presumably in America. Hakluyt did not think this was the earliest settlement of America, but men from the British Isles did contribute themselves, their culture, and their language to the population of parts of America (1907:V, 79–80).

Antonio de Herrera's *Historia general de los hechos de los castella-*

nos was a massive work. The latest editions run to seventeen volumes (Madrid, 1934–1957) and ten volumes (Asunción de Paraguay and Buenos Aires, 1944–1947). John Stevens' English translation (London, 1725–1726) was in six volumes. Herrera, as the official historian of Spain and the Indies, had access to unpublished works as well as published materials. He consulted virtually all the commentators on Indian origins, including the works of such men as Motolinía, Fernando Colón, and Las Casas, not then available in published Spanish editions.

Acosta made the greatest impact on Herrera. His argument concerning the origins of the Americans paralleled Acosta's rather closely: he rejected a second Noah's Ark and intentional voyages to America. He denied that the ancients knew of the lodestone or compass, or that they knew much about sailing. His conclusions were largely Acosta's: that which would reveal the most about the origins of the Indians was the proximity of America to parts of the Old World, but Europe's geographical knowledge was too scanty to affirm anything in that respect (1934–1957:II, 37–38).

Herrera did not follow Acosta so far as to affirm that the culture of the natives developed after they arrived in America. Consequently, he was free to speculate about the possible origins of the Indians within the geographical limitations imposed by Acosta. There were some people, Herrera noted, who said that Greenland and Estotiland (Labrador) were connected. If that were so, then people from Norway or Lapland could have come to America by an almost all-land route. (The distance between Norway and Greenland was generally greatly underestimated in the sixteenth and seventeenth centuries.) Evidence that this contact was probable could be found in certain customs common to Laplanders, Norwegians, and Estotilanders. All these peoples lived in forests, caves, or hollow trees; all clothed themselves in skins, all ate fish and wild fruit, and they differed little in color (1934–1957:II, 38).

Other men, he continued, believed Tierra del Fuego to be a part of a great antarctic continent which connected with the East Indies. If that were so, migrants could come that way with only small canoes or *balsas,* and without need of a compass. Evidence that this route might have been used lay in the common color of the natives of the East and West Indies (1934–1957:II, 38–39). Herrera did not think that there was any evidence indicating that the Indian might have descended from the more civilized parts of Europe. Anyway, he wrote, the Indians most probably came to America "because of the nearness of the land, and they expanded little by little" (1934–1957:II, 39).

The engineer Enrico Martín is probably best known for his work in draining the Valley of Mexico. He added a new element to the debate on Indian origins in his *Reportorio de los tiempos é Historia natural de Nueva España* (Mexico, 1606). Martín did not refer to Acosta by name, but his book reveals an adherence to the type of approach expounded by the old Jesuit. The Old World, he said, was easily filled up because it was all geographically contiguous. The New World posed a problem primarily because it seemed to be surrounded by broad oceans. Nevertheless, Martín thought the first settlers must surely have come to the Indies by land. The lack of the art of navigation in ancient times, and the inability of men and animals to come by air forced that conclusion on him (1606:104).

Martín suggested that a likely route for the earliest immigration would cross from Asia to America in the region of Anian—a place variously located in extreme northeastern Siberia and northwestern America. Martín did not think the supposed Strait of Anian, which many thought separated northeastern Asia from America, would be wide enough to impede either man or beast (1606:104–105). In his younger days Enrico Martín had traveled briefly in Courland (modern Estonia), and he testified that the inhabitants of Courland were people of the same "traza, color, condición, y brío" as the Indians of New Spain. He noted, however, that the Courlanders were more corpulent than the Indians. He also noted that the people of Courland differed from their neighbors in both language and color. And, he concluded, the Courlanders and Indians seemed to him to be the same people (1606:104).

Martín did not argue that the Indians were from Courland, but that they were the same type of people as the Courlanders. He may have thought that the Indians migrated to America from Courland by way of the Strait of Anian, but if so he did not make it clear. By the same token, he may have had some concept of a common origin for the Indians and the Courlanders, perhaps in Siberia. His statement concerning the racial and linguistic isolation of the Courlanders indicates that he probably did have such an idea in mind. Martín, however, did not make the idea explicit.

The geographical and faunal considerations introduced into the debate by Acosta, and the skepticism which he expressed concerning the value of the cultural comparison technique had such a great impact on later writers who considered the origins of the American Indians that this writer has distinguished an Acostan Tradition. The Acostan influence was explicit in the work of Anello Oliva and Antonio de Herrera. It was also apparent in Martín's *Reportorio*. Mendieta likewise expressed sentiments in keeping with the Acostan Tradition, but he may not have known Acosta's book.

Acosta was not the first of the "restrained" commentators. Las Casas, Landa, Román y Zamora, and Sahagún were similarly reluctant to commit themselves on the point of Indian origins. But Acosta was the first to put all the elements producing restraint into a well-thought-out argument which objectively exposed all the considerations necessary to a solution to the problem of American origins. For that reason it seemed appropriate that the "scientific" theme bear his name.

Gregorio García and the Garcían Tradition

Nowhere is the general confusion and genuine indecision of the sixteenth century theorists of Indian origins more pronounced than in Gregorio García's massive summation of the various theories: *Origen de los indios de el nuevo mundo, e Indias occidentales* (Valencia, 1607). García spent nine years in Peru, beginning in the late 1590's. He was struck by the wonders of the place: "unused waters, new air, a hitherto unseen sky, rare animals and birds; fruits, herbs, and plants never before written about." Out of this strangeness and novelty was born a great desire to know the causes of it all—especially a desire to know who the people were, and how they got there (1729: "al lector" [pp. 4–6]).

In order to discover as best he could what the origins of the Indians were, García evaluated what he read, what he was told by both Spaniards and Indians, and what he had seen. He did not quote very often, for his purpose in the *Origen* did not require it. He was primarily interested in identifying all possible sources for man in America and stating each of the arguments based on those sources as strongly as possible. Thus, for each opinion, García posed all the objections he knew, and refuted them in turn. García utilized the standard classical authorities, many biblical commentators, several "cosmographers," authors of questionable "traditional" histories (such as Berosus), and most of the Spaniards who had offered origin theories.

Before discussing the various opinions on origins, García explained the conditions which governed the development of his treatise. First it was necessary to accept three things as fundamentals on which to base the structure and the argument of the book. The first dealt with the Catholic faith: That all—

men and women had, and have, since the Beginning of the World, proceeded, and taken their beginning and origin from our first parents Adam and Eve; and subsequently from Noah and his sons, who were all who remained alive after the General Deluge . . . (1729:1);

and that Noah divided the world giving Asia to Shem, Egypt and Africa to Ham, and Europe to Japheth.

The second fundamental was:

that people now in the Indies, whom we call Indians, went to them from one of the three parts of the known world . . . The reason for this is that if the fourth part called America were inhabited at the beginning of the world, or before the Flood, in the time of Noah and his sons or grandsons, there would have been notice of it and the ancient Historians and Cosmographers would have mentioned it as they did the three said parts. But in old times they considered them uninhabited because they were below the Burning Zone. Thus we are forced to concede that the Indians went to the Indies from one of the aforementioned parts (1729:8).

And to those who remarked that it would be unreasonable to expect the ancients to know of such remote places, "I say that as Ptolomey knew of China," he would also have known of New Spain, which was near China and Greater Tatary (1729:8).

Fundamental number three concerned the ways of knowing. "All philosophers and theologians, Christian and Gentile alike, agree that all knowledge comes by one of four ways or methods": *Ciencia, Opinión, Fé Divina,* and *Fé Humana* (1729:9).

That which we know through Science is certain, true, and evident; because, as Aristotle says, we know it by its cause [lo sabemos por su causa] . . . To know [El saber] is to discover [conocer] the thing by its cause . . . we think we know when we understand [conocemos] the thing by its cause.

Whatever we know by Opinion is doubtful and uncertain because it is based on probability [procede de fundamentos probables], which may or may not be true, or false, or thought of as such; thus each one follows the Opinion which seems true to him, consistent with the reasons on which it is based . . .

and which he judges, or knows, to be true or probable. On the other hand, "whatever we know by *Fé Divina* is certain, true, and cannot be otherwise . . . because the means by which we know it is the Authority of the Catholic Church, to which our Lord God revealed it" (1729:9).

"Whatever we know by *Fé Humana* has no other basis for its truth than the Authority of whoever said it." If it is said by a "serious, faithful man whose authority we trust," we may accept what is said. But if it is said by someone of little or no authority, we should consider it false, or at least doubt that it is true. From all this we can understand the "truth of the Castillian proverb which says: 'El creer es cortesía' " (1729:9).

García still had to decide which of the four methods was applicable to the study of Indian origins. In order to determine which to use, Fray Gregorio resorted to what "the Dialecticians call *induction.*" Science he thought of no use because there was no reason or demonstration which could "engender in our Understanding, true, certain, and obvious knowledge of whence the Indians came." Nor was *Fé Divina* of any great help, because, though the Scripture taught the origin of all men from Adam and Eve, and Noah and his sons, it did not reveal which people went to the Indies (1729:9).

Fé Humana was likewise useless, because before Columbus discovered the Indies no one "made mention of them and gave us certain and true reports of them." This absence of comment in the Old World was not alleviated by American sources, because the Indians had only "fabulous" memories of their origins (1729:9–11). The only way not already excluded was *Opinión* and that was of dubious value, because one of its characteristics was that it could not provide undeniable proof. Consequently, one could choose whatever opinion seemed most true to him (1729:11–12).

García's catalogue of the "methods" of knowing was not well thought-out, nor did he abide by it consistently in his text. For one thing, the methods were not as exclusive as he indicated. Science apparently meant to García knowledge gained from demonstrating what was obvious, i.e., from common sense. The term "science" applied to both the method of acquiring knowledge and to the knowledge thus acquired. But would a "demonstration" by someone of "little or no authority" be as readily accepted as one by a man of great authority? Would not the acceptance or rejection of the report of a demonstration depend on what García called *Fé Humana?*

Opinión was even more amorphous. It seemed to be only a step below science in that its demonstrations were demonstrations of probability. If a man riding eastward across European Russia postulated the existence of a mountain range within the next one thousand miles and argued that one should be there because the plain seldom stretched so far without interruption, he would have stated an opinion—a conjecture. If he rode on to the Urals he could demonstrate a scientific fact. If the man were Aristotle and he stopped with the unproven conjecture, what weight would his opinion carry? Would Aristotle's conjecture of mountains be more probable than Sarmiento de Gamboa's conjecture of a Greek origin for the Yucatecan Indians because he thought he heard them use some Greek words?

Would the case of Sarmiento de Gamboa's report of Greek words in Yucatán properly fall within the scope of opinion? Would not the presence of Greek words in Yucatán seem highly improbable to Europeans? Would the European judge this case on the probability of its accuracy, or on the reputation of Sarmiento de Gamboa? If the latter, it would fall in the category of *Fé Humana.* It would be difficult to distinguish accurately between the two types of knowing.

Indeed, the overriding consideration seemed to be not *Opinión,* but

Fé Humana. This latter quality must of necessity influence "Science," and *Opinión.* Like Science and Opinion, *Fé Humana* appeared to have no independent existence. Acceptance of an interpretation of a literary passage could be governed by the "authority" of the interpreter. On the other hand, it could be governed on the basis of whether one thought the interpretation probable or not.

Only *Fé Divina* had a truly independent existence. Its authority was absolute, and by definition pronouncements made under its shield were true. "The difference between the Spirit of Divine Prophecy and Natural Prophecy is that the former is certain and infallible, while the latter is uncertain and fallible since it proceeds from conjecture . . ." (1729:25).

This analysis is perhaps too critical. García and his contemporaries believed in the independence of *Opinión* and *Fé Humana* as judges of proof and truth. Their understanding of *Opinión* seemed roughly this: Things which were probable, or which could be made to appear probable, were matters of *Opinión.* Acceptance or rejection depended upon whether *you* thought them probable. Things which were merely said to be so or to exist, with no attempt to substantiate the assertion, were matters for *Fé Humana,* and were to be believed or not depending on the reputation of the person making the claim. This will not satisfy the modern reader, but at least it borders on the understandable. This understanding of *Opinión* was made more nearly obvious by García's answer to Acosta's assertion that the evidence of the remnants of the Jewish language and culture in the Indies was largely conjectural. True, replied García, but the essence of *Opinión* is that it does not "have to be the most noticeable and obvious truths . . . but that they be probable, and have the appearance of truth, and be held true, even though they really are not" (1729:123).

García identified some eleven major opinions regarding the origins of the American Indians. Some of these were actually collections of related opinions, and some dealt with ways of getting to the Indies. The number of separate sources was about a dozen. García summarized the available information about the proposed theories. He also either invented a few origin theories of his own or gave the first published expression to theories current, but unpublished until 1607.

The first opinion dealt with the belief "that the first Indians went to the Indies by Sea" and that they went there knowingly because they had heard of the New World. Some writers, notably Acosta, had considered such a possibility but rejected it. García knew of Acosta's work and his objection that the Indians could not have come by design since the ancients had no compass or art of navigation with which to cross the ocean and acquire knowledge of America. García replied that the art of navigation had been invented by Noah and was therefore as old as man. García also thought that the ancients might have known the lodestone. Adam was aware of all things in nature including the lodestone, and Noah probably knew of it also. He could have passed the knowledge along to his descendants (1729:12–15).

The ancients had also made long voyages. The Jews of Solomon's time had sailed to Ophir and Tarshish, and Ophir might be in the Indies. García rejected Acosta's contention that Ophir and Tarshish were merely names for faraway places rather than specific places (1729:15–20). There was also the example of Hanno's voyage around Africa. Long voyages, therefore, had occurred in antiquity with or without the compass (1729:20–21).

Another objection to the foreknowledge of the original settlers was the absence of specific references to the New World in ancient literature (1729:21–22). García pointed out that many phrases of the ancients could be construed as references to America: Plato's Atlantis, Aristotle's Carthaginian story, Seneca's reference in *Medea*, Plutarch's Sporades (legendary islands off the coast of Britain), and certain statements in Lucian (1729:23–28). Also, he said, certain verses in Isaiah might apply to America (1729:30–31):

For I know their works and their thoughts, and I am coming to gather all nations and tongues; and they shall come and shall see my glory, and I will set a sign among them. And from them I will send survivors to the nations, to Tarshish, Put, and Lud, who draw the bow, to Tubal and Javan, to the coastlands afar off, that have not heard my fame or seen my glory; and they shall declare my glory among the nations. And they shall bring all your brethren from all nations . . . (Isaiah 66: 18–20).

García felt that the author of these passages must have known of America, "the coastlands afar off."

Since García took opinions two and three directly from Acosta, they need not be detailed. The second dealt with the possibility of men coming to the Indies as a result of a storm. García paraphrased Acosta extensively on this, and adopted his conclusion that it could have happened. The third opinion concerned the beasts and how they got to America. The arguments leading to the postulation of a land connection closely paralleled Acosta (1729:34–40).

The fourth opinion concerned the Carthaginian origin of the Indians. The discussion of this opinion diverged into various related questions which made it one of the longest sections in the *Origen*. García used the Aristotle story as his point of departure. His source for the story apparently was a late edition of Vanegas de Bustos. Aristotle had written that all the people who went to the island in the western Atlantic were killed. Vanegas proposed that some had escaped and returned to settle the island, providing the nucleus for the Indian race (1729: 41–42). García thought there was considerable evidence to support such a conjecture. From the practical point of view, if the Carthaginians sailed to Española or Cuba, then it would be no problem for them to spread to the mainland. Furthermore, they were accustomed to long voyages. On a different level of proof, the picture writing of New Spain resembled Carthaginian pictographs. García also suggested that the ruins the Spaniards discovered in Yucatán and Charcas seemed to be Carthaginian in style. Finally, he maintained that both peoples practiced child sacrifice (1729:42–50).

Numerous objections to the Carthaginian theory were posed. Why was the language of the Indians not Carthaginian? And why were there so many languages? García blamed the language pattern on the Devil. Satan helped the Indians invent new languages, knowing that a variety of languages would impede the efforts of Christian evangelists. But what of the difference in the dress of the Carthaginians and Indians? García conceded the difference, but he argued that costume varied with climate. Despite this variation among the Indians, they did have sufficient characteristics in common to indicate a common origin. All were idolators and sun-worshippers; all had priests and sacrifices; and all were inclined to drink and to lack ambition (1729:52–54).

The third objection to the Carthaginian origin applied equally to any other seaborne migration. How did the sailors get animals to the New World? The question was complicated by the fact that America possessed not only Old World species, but also some unique animals, such as the llama, the alpaca, and the vicuña, which were unknown to the ancients. "I confess," wrote García (1729:54), "that this doubt and objection is of such difficulty that I have burdened my mind with it for many years."

The Old World species might have come by land, as Acosta argued; but, if there were a land connection, why postulate a trans-Atlantic migration? Perhaps the settlers brought the animals in their ships for sport. That was possible, but unsatisfactory, because it did not explain the vast variety of animals which could not be used for sport. But most important, it did not explain the *animales peregrinas,* the unique animals. A land bridge would not explain those creatures either, unless one followed Acosta and supposed that entire species migrated to separate parts of the world after the Flood. But García was operating temporarily within the limits imposed by a trans-Atlantic migration and had to explain the unique fauna on the assumption that they could have come exclusively by ship (1729:54–55).

Had God made a new creation after the Flood? Possibly; but the Scripture would not support such an assumption. So one must assume that:

they proceed from some species of wild and domestic animals that are in Africa, Asia, and Europe, which passed to the Indies by water, or land . . . but that due to the disposition of the Earth, and *particular influencia,* and the constellations of the heavens, or other causes . . . they acquired accidental differences and became Monsters and thus seem unique (1729:56–57).

García knew that monsters did happen—witness such "monsters" as men born with one leg, hermaphrodites, and midgets—and there was a well established tradition about monsters (1729:57–64). With this in mind, García suggested that the llama might be a monster of the camel species (1729:63). But this posed another problem. Monsters were generally anomalies. They appeared at random and were recognized by some drastic difference between themselves and their parents. Furthermore, monsters did not breed true, if they bred at all. Descend-

ants of monsters should theoretically revert to the characteristic physique of their species (1729:64).

Since the *animales peregrinas* of South America did breed true and
did resemble their parents, it would seem that they could not be monsters. García proposed that, just as an individual might be a monster
in his species, an entire line might be a monster *to* its species. He distinguished two types of monstrosity. One resulted from the union of
parents different in species. The other came from the union of parents
of the same species as a consequence of personal, natural, or stellar de-
fects at the instant of conception. Because the circumstances surrounding its creation were of so powerful a nature, "the second, although not
monsters with respect to individuals or to their parents, are with respect to the [original] species." The first type would cease to be monsters after the third generation because "those of the first type are now
of a third species *(otra specie tercera)* different from those of their
parents; but those of the second type," since they came from two members of the same species, "do not change species" but remain monsters
to the parent species (1729:64).

García decided that the rare animals of Peru were not currently monsters after all. They were *animales mestizos* which arose through the
union of separate known species (1729:66–68). There were other solutions to the problem of unique fauna. They might be subsumed under Old World types. For example, the "sheep" of Peru might be a
species of camel. On the other hand, God may have assigned different
species to various parts of the world and arranged to transport them
there after the Deluge (1729:66–68).

How fixed was the idea of "fixity of species" when animals of different species could give rise to a third species, and animals of the same
species could give rise to monsters which bred true and produced what
was in effect (though not admitted) a different species?

García had one last objection to the Carthaginian theory to dispose
of. Why did the Indians not have beards like the Carthaginians? He
answered that the climate of the Indies was of such a nature that men
lost their facial hair. Carthaginians, who were from a warm climate
anyway, were more prone to the loss of hair than were Spaniards who
came from a cooler climate. The hair on a man's head was not affected

because it was there at birth. Only hair which developed after birth would be affected (1729:69–78).

Until 1607 the theory of a Jewish origin for the Indians had not played a dominant role in the literature. Several writers used it, but as many had rejected as had accepted it. This theory, however, probably enjoyed a greater popularity among laymen than among the writers. And if the importance or popularity of a theory were judged by the space García devoted to it, the Hebrew theory (or theories) would seem paramount. García himself testified to the popularity of the theory among the common people of America, who, he said, thought the Indians descended from the tribes of Hebrews lost in the Captivity of Shalmaneser. They based their belief in the condition, nature, and customs of the Indians, which they thought similar to the condition, nature, and customs of the Hebrews (1729:79).

García admitted that he had spent more time pondering this subject than any of the other theories, because he wanted to be sure to phrase it as well and as strongly as possible. He decided to use Gilbert Genebrard as his chief literary source for the opinion (1729:79). Genebrard's evidence was largely circumstantial: rumors of graves in the Azores with Hebrew writing on them; old traditions of Jews being surrounded, as they were in America, by water; and, of course, cultural comparisons and biblical or pseudo-biblical authority (1729: 79–80).

The fullest statement of the Ten Lost Tribes theory relied on the apocryphal IV Esdras. The story of the journey to Arsareth was presented in full in the discussion of Suárez de Peralta. Many writers identified Arsareth as America. But if that were the case, what route did the Hebrews take to America? García proposed two routes. One would have the tribes pass through Tatary and the lands of the Mongols to the Straits of Anian where they could pass over into the Kingdom of Anian, which García placed in North America. During their journey they acquired a few customs from the Tatars, such as sun-worshipping (1729:80–81). The alternate route ran through China to the Strait of Anian (1729:81–82).

Acosta had made some rather pointed criticisms of the Lost Tribe theory. Esdras, he observed, was apocryphal, and one did not have to believe it. Furthermore, the Esdras vision specifically stated that the Tribes went to Arsareth to keep their law. The Indians did not practice Jewish law. García circumvented that objection by asserting that some Indians had not lived up to their intentions (1729:127–128). The other strong objection came from the Bible itself. II Kings 17:6 asserted that King Shalmaneser scattered the tribes in the cities of the Medes and other places. García responded that some had stayed there, but most had gone on as Esdras reported in his vision (1729:82–84).

The Esdras story merely indicated that the Jews could have come to America. To prove that they had come, it was necessary to find cultural traits common to the Indians and the Hebrews of the Ten Lost Tribes. That proved easy. Both peoples were timid, prone to ceremony and idolatry, and liars. When the Scripture spoke of Jewish heroism, it referred to the Tribe of Judah, not the Ten Lost ones. In this initial comparison (1729:84–85), García closely paralleled Diego Durán (1951:I, 1); but there is no evidence he used Durán's manuscript.

García illustrated the timidity and passivity of the Indians by referring to the ease with which the Spaniards conquered them (1729:86–87). Other alleged similarities were cited: big noses, guttural speech, incredulity, ingratitude, lack of charity, and use of sleeveless robes (1729:86–93). In times of stress, he remarked, both Indians and Jews lift their arms up to Heaven. Both call their relatives of the second and third degree of consanguinity brothers; both bury their dead away in the hills; rend their clothes when despairing; sacrifice children; use drugs or wine; and kiss the cheek as a sign of love or peace (1729:93–100).

What happened to Jewish learning if the Indians were Jews? Why had they forgotten their writing and become rude, stupid, ugly, and of such low esteem? And if the Indians were Jewish, what was their responsibility in connection with the death of Christ?

The answers to these questions were manifold. First, the good things attributed to the Jews—bravery, learning, and high esteem—probably applied only to the tribes of Judah or Benjamin. The other ten tribes were inferior in culture. Secondly, the diet and climate of America produced variations in intelligence and accomplishment which made the Indians seem un-Jewish. Furthermore, God probably ordained that men of differing regions also differ in character. There were, after all, some intelligent Indians. As for the association with the death of Christ, the Indians were innocent because they left Israel long before that event (1729:100–106).

García then offered another reason why the Indians had no writing. This aspect of the investigation applied to all theories. Since Adam probably invented writing, he observed, why were there *any* illiterate peoples? In the case of the Indians, the loss of writing probably occurred during the long journey, or because of some disaster (1729: 106–108).

The question why the Indians failed to observe Mosaic law as the Jews did everywhere else still remained. García's contention that their intention did not match their action was incomplete. The answer lay in the character of the Ten Tribes. The Bible (RSV, II Kings 17:7–17) clearly indicated that the "lost" tribes were disposed to evil and idolatry. This disposition no doubt was strengthened by contact with such peoples as the Tatars and Mongols during the journey to Arsareth (1729:108–109). Actually, the Indians did appear to keep certain parts of the law in certain areas. The Incas held a festival in March similar to the Passover; the Yucatecan Indians practiced circumcision; Mexicans and Incas had eternal altar fires; some Nicaraguans would not allow women who had recently given birth into the temples. Other parts of the law observed at various places included those which said that men should not sleep with women who had recently given birth; if a master slept with a slave both were whipped; adultresses were to be stoned; men and women must not wear each other's clothes; and a widow must marry her nearest male relative. The Decalogue was not kept very well in the Indies, but one could find parts of it observed in various places (1729:109–117).

The last few objections to the Jewish thesis received extensive treatment. The Indians did not speak Hebrew because languages were developed so easily after Babel that a group could readily create its own. The Indians did retain a few Hebrew words such as Yucatán (Iectan), Mexico (mesico), and Peru (fertile). As for Acosta's observation that the Indians did not value silver, García replied that they did not need it (1729:117–124).

Ophir did not receive a fifth the attention devoted to the Jews. García took his version from Arias Montano, but buttressed it with references to Genebrard. He owed nothing to Cabello Valboa, whose work he did not seem to know; but his version departs from Cabello Valboa's in few ways. García fused the two types of Ophirian tradition by having the Ophirians develop in the Far East and then go to Peru with Solomon's fleet. The elephants and ivory associated with the story were acquired en route in the East Indies (1729:129–141).

Atlantis could also have provided the American population. The proof of the Atlantis thesis lay in the story of Plato, in Aristotle's assertion that the Atlantic Ocean was shallow, and in the retention of the word "atl" (water) by the Mexicans (1729:140–144). García dismissed the objections to Atlantis by asserting that Plato wrote history, not fable, when he spoke of the island. Furthermore, when Plato said Atlantis was larger than Asia and Africa combined, he referred to the much smaller areas to which those names applied in antiquity. The date of the drowning of Atlantis—nine thousand years before Plato—seemed to place the event before the Flood; but Plato, said García, may have used a year of shorter length (1729:144–157).

But what of Plato's contention that all on Atlantis had drowned? If that were so, how could Atlanteans have settled the Indies? And was there any cultural evidence that the Indians were Atlanteans? García responded that the Indians went to America before the catastrophe. Anyway, certain islands too insignificant to require notice had survived the inundation. Furthermore, in both Peru and Atlantis the first-born prince succeeded to the throne, the people worshiped golden idols and used copper, and held land in common (1729:158–163).

García even resurrected the old theory of a Spanish derivation for the Indians which no one had taken seriously since Oviedo proposed it in 1535. He identified three variants to the Spanish theory. He borrowed one from Oviedo, one from López de Gómara, and apparently invented the other. He discussed the Oviedo version first. García added (1729:163–173) that certain similarities not mentioned by Oviedo (such as crudeness, lack of government, false religions, barbarousness, opposition to science) supported the Hesperian theory.

The second variant held that the Indians came to America after the sinking of Atlantis and during the time of Roman influence in Spain. The domestic dog, the love of vermilion, the Quechua language, the *mitayo,* divination by looking at the entrails of animals, use of temple (vestal) virgins, and the Inca roads all showed Romanized-Spanish influence (1729:173–187).

The third variant, which López de Gómara rejected, placed the migration from Spain to the Indies after the fall of Rome and after the development of the Castilian language. Most likely this occurred after 711 A.D. when the Moors defeated King Rodrigo. García included this migration theory because there were many word similarities between Spanish and the Indian languages—especially Quechua (1729:187–189).

The possibility of a Greek ancestry for the Indians must also be explored. The Greeks were, after all, the first to learn navigation after Noah. Also certain words used in Yucatán, as Sarmiento de Gamboa had reported, seemed to be Greek. Although he had to consider this possibility, García could find only enough evidence to fill four pages (1729:189–192).

García distinguished between the Carthaginian theory and a Phoenician origin; most other writers used the terms interchangeably. To do so he had to read the Phoenicians into the Aristotelian story of the uninhabited island, and to credit Vanegas with a distinction between Phoenicians and Carthaginians. Both attributions were unwarranted (1729: 192–193).

The last theory García identified dealt with the East Asian origin possibilities. Chinese, Tatars, Scythians, and other East Asians were lumped together. García thought the proximity of the Chinese homeland to America might have led them to migrate there, and he found various similarities in peoples and customs to support this idea (1729: 239–247). He noted the physical resemblances of Chinese and Indians: facial features, physique, color, and lack of beard. On the cultural level, he observed that both worshiped the sun as a god, both were idolatrous, both used lunar months and knotted cords, and in both China and the Indies there was a rare law allowing nephews rather than sons to inherit property. Since García identified the other East Asian peoples with the Chinese, he did not include a separate discussion of them (1729:247).

These were the only legitimate opinions concerning the origins of the American Indians García could discover in 1607. He did allude to a few blasphemous opinions for the purpose of denouncing them. He attributed to Avicenna and Andrés Cisalpino an "insane" belief that men may have arisen from decaying matter. He thought those who would form men by alchemy were equally mad (1729:248).

Gregorio García's *Origen de los indios de el nuevo mundo* is one of the most widely quoted and most generally misunderstood books in origin literature. This situation arises largely from the failure of his readers—especially modern ones—to grasp the fact that his purpose was not to prove any one opinion as against any other, but *to prove them all.* "From the fact that at one place I prove that the Ancients did know of America and in another place I prove they did not, it might seem that I contradict myself," he said. "But this is not the case. On the one hand I write as the author of the entire work" and on the other "as a particular author and a partisan of this first opinion" (1729:33).

García's purpose was again pointed up when it became necessary for him to state his own conclusion. He was reluctant to do so. In the end he rejected all the theories separately, and affirmed them all collectively: The Indians—

proceed neither from one Nation or people, nor went to those parts from one [part] of the Old World. Nor did the first settlers all walk or sail by the same road or voyage nor in the same time, nor in the same manner. But actually they proceeded from various nations, from which some came by sea, forced and driven by storms; others by art of navigation looking for those lands, of which they had heard. Some came by land . . . (1729:315).

Father Gregorio's inability to reject any of these professed opinions, and his decision to accept all the varieties of opinion may indeed reflect merely his own values. Yet these values were characteristic of the writings of many of the commentators before, and especially after, his *Origen.* Few Europeans in 1607 could, or would, follow Acosta to the conclusion that cultural similarities were useless in determining the relation of one people to another. Few would, or could, believe in the possibility of autocthonous development of culture even in so isolated a place as America. What Margaret Hodgen called "similarities and their documentary properties" was essential to Europe in its attempts to understand not merely the New World of America, but also the new worlds of sub-Saharan Africa and distant Asia. All the new peoples of the world had somehow to be accounted for; their ancestry had to be traced to recognized biblical lines; their cultures had to be explained to Europeans in European terms. And Europe's concept of cultural variety was highly limited (Hodgen, 1964:49–74, 202–251).

Since all men descended from Adam and secondarily from Noah, all had originally possessed common cultural traits. Some differentiation was discernible in biblical tradition, and much was discoverable in the ancient writings. Several varieties of cultures were well established in the biblical and antique record. Cosmographers and commentators of Medieval and Renaissance Europe kept them current. But these "modern" authorities on world cultures got their information largely from antique sources, and kept alive the illusion that descriptions valid in Aristotle's or Strabo's time were still valid (Hodgen, 1964:17–74).

In much writing of the time there was implicit assumption that cultural change for primitive peoples virtually stopped before the time of Christ. Thus all modern cultures could be traced to their sources by comparing them with the classic literary forms. There was little understanding that certain cultural traits might produce comparisons more valid than others. Indiscriminate comparison was the general practice. Comparison of language, dress, religious ideas (on the most superficial of levels, such as noting the presence or absence of idols), and kinship forms were the only tools the cosmographer-ethnographer possessed. In all probability, he would consider the type of clothing more important than kinship systems in documenting connections. The superficial comparison of words, though it generally did recognize that similar sound and meaning were essential for a valid comparison, was a far cry from the linguistic comparisons of later centuries.

The cosmographer-ethnologist needed his comparative technique; he had no other method. He could not grant autocthony to cultures because that would destroy his method. Anyway, there were few people who genuinely believed autocthony possible, or who even thought of the possibility.

Actually the method itself was not quite as bad as some of its practitioners. And the practice was impeded by a lack of accurate reporting, as well as by the tendency to accept ancient testimony as applicable to modern situations. But the accuracy and volume of the information on new peoples was increasing; the ancients would be quoted less frequently in the future than in the past.

Another characteristic of the comparative technique—at least as it was practiced throughout the sixteenth and seventeenth centuries—was that though similarities were considered indicative of relationship, dissimilarities were considered irrelevant, if noticed at all. This was nowhere more evident than in the *Origen de los indios* of Gregorio García.

García was no pacesetter. His book was full of incorrect information which he could have avoided had he been genuinely capable of judging the validity of ancient and contemporaneous reports; or had he been able to remember that Castilian proverb "El creer es cortesía," and had viewed his informants with a measure of skepticism. So well did García illustrate the uncritical use of the comparative technique in connection with the search for the origins of the American Indians, that he justly deserves to have named for him that tradition characterized by credulity in its treatment of materials, uncritical acceptance of possible origins, a tendency to favor trans-Atlantic migrations, and a general inability to judge the value of various opinions with skepticism. He did not invent the attitude; but he was its greatest exemplar. That is the Garcían Tradition.

CHAPTER III

Spanish Scholarship after García, 1607–1729

S PANISH SCHOLARS dominated the controversy over the origins of the American Indians in the sixteenth century. Until 1609 only a few Portuguese writers such as Galvão and Magalhães, and a handful of North Europeans had contributed much to the argument. Of all the non-Spaniards who took part in the debate, only the Frenchman Gilbert Genebrard reached a wide audience. The dominance of Spanish scholarship in this specialized area merely reflected the general dominance by Spanish writers of the whole literature on America. A few Frenchmen, such as Thevet and Lery, and some Germans, such as Schmidel and Federman, wrote accounts of their travels in America. Englishmen such as Gage and Hakluyt also contributed to the literature on America.

Most of the non-Spanish material reflected the result of a passing acquaintance with America. No comprehensive review of American problems such as those by Oviedo, or Acosta, or Herrera came from the Northern writers, largely because of the political dominance by Spain in the areas of high culture in America. The uncivilized tribes of Brazil did not arouse the imagination of the Portuguese in the way that Peru, Mexico, and Yucatán excited the Spaniards. Even after Spain's dominance of America began to weaken after 1600, the Dutch, British, French, and other Northerners who came to the New World found no civilizations comparable to those of Spanish-America. Perhaps this fact helps explain why the Northerners never produced the monumental surveys of native America so characteristic of Spanish-American historiography. Only Spanish-America possessed the indigenous materials necessary to the composition of heroic histories.

The northern Europeans who went to America in increasing numbers after 1600 faced the same ethnological problems that the Spaniards had worried with for a century. Their approach to a solution of these problems—among them the question of Indian origins—did not differ greatly from that used by Spanish scholars. Since many Northern scholars had no access to Spanish works on the subject, the new European commentators frequently "rediscovered" theories that the Spanish had toyed with for generations.

The attitude of the north Europeans proved less rigid in the long run than that of the Spaniards. But this fortunate circumstance resulted not so much from the inherent superiority of their approach as from the fact that the Northerners could borrow from the finest Spanish scholarship. By a fortuitous circumstance Edward Grimston made Joseph de Acosta's *Historia natural y moral de las Indias* available to the English reading public in 1604, on the eve of the mushrooming of English interest in the New World and in the origins of the Indians. The Acostan Tradition entered the English literature on the origins of the American Indians at the inception of English interest in the subject. By similar fortune, Joannes de Laet, who disputed vigorously with Hugo Grotius on the subject of Indian origins in the 1640's, adopted and popularized the Acostan Tradition on the Continent.

The Acostan Tradition, the finest result of Spanish scholarship on the subject of the origins of the American Indians, passed readily into the heritage of the Northern commentators. It did not achieve the same degree of influence in Spain itself, but it nonetheless remained strong throughout the first half of the seventeenth century. Most of Acosta's countrymen, however, largely ignored the implications of his arguments—especially after mid-century—and followed the pattern of the *Origen de los indios*. Spanish scholarship developed in almost total ignorance of developments outside Spain in the seventeenth century. Furthermore, despite the vitality of the Acostan Tradition, the Garcían mode of thought and investigation prevailed in Spain—especially after 1650.

If Spanish scholarship stagnated, the reason may have been that García had done his job too well. Acosta's arguments, if followed, would lead to a search for new criteria or a refinement of the old. García, if followed, would lead to an uncritical acceptance of the old information and method and a growing isolation from the mainstream of European scholarship. In 1729 Andrés Barcia republished the *Origen de los indios* with considerable additions. These additions consisted primarily of expanded arguments for old theories and extensive expositions on newer ones. The Garcían Tradition largely dominated the interim. Spanish scholarship worked itself into a backwater in the late seventeenth and early eighteenth centuries, but this development is of interest both in itself and as a contrast to Northern developments.

The first few studies of America after García consisted of attempts to complete the history of the Indians as told by themselves. The period 1608–1613 saw four major efforts in this direction. Francisco de Avila published his *Tratado y relación de los errores, falsos dioses y otras supersticiones . . . de Huarochiri* (a province of Peru) at Lima in 1608. At about the same time the Mexican Indian, Fernando de Alva Ixtlilxóchitl, began his history of the Toltecs and Chichemecs, but he did not publish it. Another Indian, the Inca Juan Santa Cruz Pachacuti, completed his likewise unpublished *Relación de antigüedades deste reyno del Perú* in 1613. In the meantime a third Indian, the Inca Garcilaso de la Vega, wrote and published his *Commentarios reales* (Part I in 1609; Part II in 1610).

The works of the Indian authors are distinguished chiefly by their individuality. Garcilaso de la Vega wrote his history primarily from Spanish sources, since his personal contact with his homeland ceased in his teens. The Mexican Ixtlilxóchitl concerned himself only with the Toltec creation myth. Santa Cruz Pachacuti merely affirmed the Trinity and the Adamic descent of the natives of Tahuanitsuyo (1927:130). Garcilaso satisfied himself with a denial that the word "Peru" even existed in the Quechua language (1945:I, 17–18). Avila went a little further than the other Indian writers. He insisted that Adam was the father of all the Indians and denied the settlement of the New World before the Flood (1942:26–28).

The influence of these works lay largely in their use by other writers. Though Spain did not dominate the discussion of Indian origins after 1600, her scholars continued their long interest in the subject. Discussion of the question touched on all the old theories catalogued by García, and on several that he had missed. Most of the theories found at least one supporter in the seventeenth century. Most of the commentators simply ignored the Atlantean theory of Indian origins, and none accepted it. Juan de Solórzano y Pereyra, in his *Disputationem de indiarum* (Spanish expansion as *Política indiana*, 1647) of 1629 referred to Atlantis as an "incredible, in my opinion fabulous, narration" (1703:4). Juan de Villagutierre Sotomayor called it a "fabulous invention" in his manuscript *Historia de la conquista de la provincia de Itzá* of 1701 (1701:5).

The commentators did not ignore the possibility of a Carthaginian source for the Americans as frequently as they ignored Atlantis. Nonetheless, this once widely accepted theory had few supporters. In his *Monarchía indiana* of 1613, Juan de Torquemada rejected the probability of either a Carthaginian or Phoenician origin. He did not believe in the possibility of voyages of a magnitude sufficient to people all America; nor did he think the animals came by ship (1723:I, 28–29). On the other hand, Pedro Simón and Bernardo de Lizana did not share Juan de Torquemada's skepticism. The Franciscan Simón, in his *Noticias historiales de las conquistas de Tierra Firme en las Indias Occidentales* (Cuenca, 1627), accepted the truth of Aristotle's story. He varied from Aristotle's version to the extent of claiming that the Carthaginians did not forget about the island. On the contrary, they later returned with women to settle the place. This return voyage also included some *animales bravos* (such as tigers and wolves) which they brought for sporting purposes (1627:33–36). Lizana, in his manuscript *Historia y conquista espiritual de Yucatán* of 1633, also accepted the Carthaginian theory; he erroneously reported that Solórzano advocated it (1892:4).

In 1638, Antonio de la Calancha devoted two chapters of his *Corónica moralizada del orden de San Agustín en el Perú con sucesos egenplares en esta monarquía* to the subject of American origins. Calancha (1638:41) simply dismissed the Carthaginian thesis. Pedro Cubero Sebastián (1684:102–107) also curtly rejected the Carthaginian possibility in his *Descripción general del mundo;* so did Alonso de Zamora (1945:I, 95–96) in his *Historia de la provincia de San Antonio del Nuevo Reino de Granada* (Barcelona, 1701). In 1711, the anonymous author of the manuscript *Isagoge,* who held to the Ophirian origin theory, accepted the Carthaginian theory as a secondary source of population. The author asserted that the "statues, buildings, and characters [pictographs]" of Guatemala testified that the Carthaginians settled in the region (1935:76–77). On the other hand, Diego López Cogolludo (1688:177) in his *Historia de Yucathan* completed about 1659 and published in 1688, thought there was no historical evidence for a Carthaginian or Phoenician origin for the ruins.

No one in the period 1607–1729 supported the Romanized-Spanish theory reported by García. This writer found only one reference to it in the literature: a curt dismissal by Calancha (1638:41). As for the separate Phoenician origin theory, Montesinos (1886:19–20) mentioned it in the 1640's, but only as a secondary influence.

One reason that the Spanish scholars of the seventeenth century generally rejected the Atlantean, Carthaginian-Phoenician, and Roman origin theories was that they did not think that the ancients knew of the New World. Torquemada (1723:I, 5–15) pointed out that the ancients could not have known of America because they knew of only three worlds—Asia, Africa, and Europe. America constituted a fourth world in an area the ancients thought did not exist. Pedro Simón, although accepting the Carthaginians, somewhat contradictorily argued for the newness of America because no one in the Old World had any definite information about it before 1492. Simón also thought America deserved the name "New World" because of the unique fauna, pygmies, giants, and other novelties it possessed (1627:3–9). Solórzano (1703:4–9) took the same line of argument; and Villagutierre (1701: 1–8) agreed with Solórzano.

The other writers generally did not discuss the question whether the ancients knew of America; but seldom did anyone adopt a theory that required such knowledge.

The Ophirian theory of Indian origins did not necessarily entail a knowledge of America by the ancients. No one supported the suggestion that the journey to Ophir in the time of Solomon might have resulted in settlement. Only the non-Judaic version of the Ophirian theory received much support in the seventeenth century; the commentators used the Solomonic reference only to illustrate that Ophir already existed in the time of Solomon. The theory had no great appeal; this writer has found only two authors who seriously considered it in the intra-Garcían period.

Fernando de Montesinos gave the Ophirian theory its first support after 1607 in his manuscript *Ophir de España: Memórias antiguas historiales y políticas del Perú,* completed around 1644. Book II appeared first in French in 1840, Spanish in 1870, and English in 1920. Book I remains unpublished. Markham roundly condemned Montesinos as a "credulous and uncritical . . . literary pirate" (Montesinos, 1920:14); and Philip A. Means regarded his *Memorias antiguas* as "the mutilated form of the perfectly sound *Vocabulario histórico"* of Blas Valera (Montesinos, 1920:xv).

Though Montesinos probably did use Blas Valera's work, he wrote the Ophirian sections himself. The author had many idiosyncracies, such as the puzzling and amusing insistence on referring to America as "Hamérica." Marcos Jiménez de la Espada said he did this because he thought the name "was not derived from Amérigo, but was a mysterious anagram for 'Hec Maria,' the Mother of Christ" (Montesinos, 1930:5n.).

The first book, containing "Biblical and astrological matter of no value" (1920:xi), presumably laid the basis for Book II. When the published version takes up, Ophir (a great-great-great grandson of Noah, identified by Montesinos as a grandson) had already settled the New World: "After settling Hamérica, Ophir instructed his sons and grandsons in the fear of God and observance of natural law" (1930: 3). Fortunately, Montesinos recapitulated much of his argument. He thought that the first people had arrived in "Hamérica" soon after the

Flood. Population pressure in Armenia, where the Ark landed, forced Noah to send his descendants away. Some went to America; Noah may also have made the trip (1930:5–6, 15).

An excerpt from Book I, summarizing Montesinos' opinion on the first settlers of America, appeared in the 1882 edition of Book II.

Speaking with the modesty due when treating of a matter hidden in Holy Scripture and unknown for so long before our century: I say that Ophir, grandson of Noah, and his descendants populated Peru and the rest of Hamérica. They came from the East, establishing their settlements as far as Peru—the end of the world so far as the voyagers were concerned. Here, seeing its great wealth of gold, silver, and precious stones, pearls, woods, animals, and beautiful birds, they fixed their name and founded their great cities. Events of later times brought various peoples there—Tyrians, Phoenicians, and diverse other nations who came in their fleets, and they populated almost all these extensive provinces (1882:19–20).

This theory differed from previous Ophirian theses. Prior adherents had held that Ophir settled in the Far East and his descendants in America. Montesinos brought Ophir himself to the Indies; he also pushed back the date of original settlement by making Ophir a grandson, rather than a great-great-great grandson, of Noah.

The most extensive endorsement of the Ophirian theory in the period appeared in 1684 when Pedro Cubero Sebastian published his book *Descripción general del mundo y notables sucessos dél* at Naples. The argument of this book requires no explanation, for it is identical with Cabello Valboa's argument. As a matter of fact the sections of Cubero (1684:96–234) dealing with the early Indians in the New World were plagiarized from Cabello Valboa. Chapters XVI–XXXV of Cubero's *Descripción* correspond directly to Cabello Valboa's Part II, Chapters 3–18, 20, and Part III, Chapters 4–6 (Cabello Valboa, 1951:92–189, 195–240). A preliminary investigation by this writer indicates that the entire *Descripción* was plagiarized from Cabello Valboa.

Although Cabello Valboa's elaborate Ophirian theory finally got into print by way of this plagiarism,, few Spaniards accepted it. Most writers of the period ignored it, or as Solórzano (1703:11–12) had done earlier, rejected it. A theory somewhat similar to the Ophirian with respect to the time of the first settlement and the "gentilidad" of the first settlers appeared in the late seventeenth century. Lucas Fernández de Piedrahita (1688:1–4), who in general belonged to the Acostan school, wrote in his *Historia general de las conquistas del Nuevo Reyno de Granada* (1688) that he thought Noah gave America to his son Japheth as part of his share of the world. Consequently, Fernández (1688:8) argued, the Indians descended from Japheth. Fernández de Piedrahita did not elaborate this idea, but Alonso de Zamora (1945:I, 97), who likewise neglected to explain the theory, adopted it on the testimony of Fernández. Other writers, except Calancha (1638:43), who had his own uses for it, failed to notice this origin theory.

Expectedly, the Ten Lost Tribes of Israel theory received the most frequent comment. It also developed some new phases. Many comments consisted merely of brief references. Pedro de Villagomes, Archbishop of Lima, wrote in his *Exortaciones e instrucción acerca de las idolatrías de los indios del Arzobispado de Lima* (Lima, 1649) of the Indians "who are all gentiles, and they were thus before being discovered by the Spaniards" (1919:11). The phrase seems to impute a non-Hebraic origin to the Indians, but there is cause to doubt that interpretation. Spaniards commonly referred to non-Christians as "gentiles." Everyone, including unconverted Indians, who had no recognizable religion, fell into this "gentile" category. The Archbishop may have meant only that the Indians "are all non-Christian"; it seems unlikely that he would have called them "non-Christian" if he thought them Jews, but seventeenth century usage of the concept of "gentilidad" does not exclude such a possibility.

Alonso de Zamora stated his position just as briefly but more explicitly. He rejected the Ten Lost Tribes theory because he thought that the descendants of Japheth had peopled America before the "Captivity" (1945:96). Most Spanish scholars of this period devoted considerable attention to the investigation of the Lost Tribes theory.

Juan de Torquemada typified the consideration given to this theory by seventeenth-century Spanish commentators. After reciting the Esdras-based argument for the theory, he concluded (1723:I, 23–25),

"I am not convinced that these Indians are those Tribes." In the first place, he observed, Esdras lacked authority. Despite the testimony of that apocryphal book, excellent evidence existed to indicate that the Ten Tribes never left the cities of the Medes. Even if one granted the truth of the Esdras story, it did not prove the identity of Arsareth and America. Then, paraphrasing Acosta, he asked why was it that "only in these Indies have the Jews forgotten their Language, their Law, their ceremonies, their Messiahs, and finally, all their Judaism?"

Torquemada did not believe that the languages of the Indians showed any definite evidences of Hebraic influence. He also concluded that native customs revealed no Jewish characteristics (1723:I, 26–27). Calancha, writing twenty-five years later, in 1638, faced in the same manner the problem of possible Indian descent from the lost Hebrew tribes, and reached a similar conclusion (1638:39–41). He did add a few wrinkles to the anti-Lost Tribes argument. For example, he contested the reliability of the vision of Esdras because he thought it improbable that King Shalmaneser of Assyria would allow the captive tribes to leave (1638:40).

Calancha also recounted a curious little story about someone who claimed that evidence of a Jewish derivation appeared in the words "Indio" and "Iudio." If one turned the "n" in "Indio" upside down, he produced the word "Iudio"! (1638:39). (The use of "I" or "J" to spell "Judio" depended on the particular author. The same held true for Englishmen who indiscriminately spelled "Jew" as "Iew" or "Iewe." Calancha thought the whole thing absurd since the "Indios" did not call themselves by that name.

Neither Torquemada nor Calancha could accept the authenticity of the Ten Lost Tribes theory. Yet the anonymous author of *Isagoge* of 1711 accepted the story of Esdras to the extent of calling America "Arsareth" throughout his manuscript. He traced the Tribes to Arsareth through Tatary, and settled them in America north of the Isthmus of Tehuántepec (1935:54–60). Carthaginians and, possibly, Egyptians produced the civilizations of Guatemala (1935:76–77, 60–67). He also hinted that Spaniards may have settled in South America (1935: 77).

Between 1607 and 1729 only one Spaniard, the author of the *Isa-*

goge, accepted the traditional version of the Ten Lost Tribes of Israel theory. A variant reading of the thesis advanced by Pedro Simón in 1627 enjoyed as much popularity and more notoriety. Simón accepted part of the Esdras story and argued that the Indians probably originated in Israel, but "only from the Tribe of Issachar." He based this belief on the prophecy of Issachar's father, Jacob (1627:37): "Issachar is a strong ass, crouching between the sheepfolds; he saw that a resting place was good, and that the land was pleasant; so he bowed his shoulder to bear, and became a slave at forced labor" (RSV, Gen. 49:14). There is a significant difference between the modern version and the rendition by Simón and others who used the Issachar story. According to Simón, Issachar "ha de estar echado entre terminos." Vazquez de Espinosa (1948:18), who adopted the Issachar theory in the portion of his *Compendio y descripción de las Indias Occidentales* published in 1630, phrases it thusly: "Isachar, asno fuerte el que haze assiento entre terminos."

The critical difference between the seventeenth century readings and the modern version is the use of the term "sheepfold" in the Revised Standard Version, whereas the early Spaniards used the undefined "entre términos"—within boundaries. Simón (1627:37–40) interpreted this prophecy to mean that Issachar would need the strength of an ass to reach his destined land where he would have to live "entre términos" in a good and pleasant place, and work as a slave, and pay tribute. This prophecy accurately mirrored the condition of the Indians: their journey to America had been an arduous one, and their station in life doomed them to carry the burdens of their conquerors, the Spaniards. The statement also correctly reflected the stolidity of the American and his ability to live like a burro at a subsistence level. The "entre términos" referred to the geographical position of America as an island surrounded by water and bounded by the Tropics—God's limits to the wanderings of the sun. Since the condition of the Indians of America corresponded to the prophesied status of Issachar's descendants, they must have descended "only from the Tribe of Issachar."

Solórzano (1629), Calancha (1638) and Zamora (1701) all analyzed the Issachar variation and rejected it. Solórzano attributed the theory to one Ruíz Bejarán, not knowing of Simón's work which was published two years earlier (Cuenca, 1627). This writer did not find any work by Ruíz Bejarán applicable to this subject. Solórzano merely catalogued the theory, but did not openly reject it. He did implicity reject it, however, by endorsing a Far Eastern non-Jewish origin (1703:11).

Calancha, with characteristic candor, referred to the Issachar story as "silly" because it would fit not only the Indians, but also Christians under Moslem control, and Negroes in Europe (1638:39–40). Zamora similarly dismissed the idea, because the Indians had lived without masters for many generations before the Spanish conquest (1945: I, 97). It should be noted in fairness to Simón, that neither Calancha nor Zamora considered all aspects of Simón's thesis. They concentrated their attention on the "condition of servitude" part of Simón's argument.

The Issachar variant was also accepted by Antonio Vazquez de Espinosa in his *Compendio* (1630). Generally, Vazquez' (1948:10–16) argument concerning the possible ways the first settlers could have come to America paralleled Acosta's; but his conclusion owes nothing to Acosta: "I say . . . that the first settlers of the Indies descended from *la mejor gente* then existing in the world, that is, from the ten Tribes of Israel, when King Salmanasar exiled them to uninhabited lands . . . and in particular from the Tribe of Isacar . . ." (1948:17–18). Without quoting any source other than the Bible and the apocryphal Esdras, Vazquez (1948:18–19) developed the Issachar theory precisely as did Simón.

Vazquez used the Lost Tribes theory to buttress his Issachar theory, with a degree of confusion resulting. Vasquez (1948:20) used the Esdras story of the migration of the Ten Lost Tribes to show how the descendants of Issachar, who were among the exiles, could have got to America—an event he dated at 739 B.C. Yet Vazquez (1948:21) continued with a discussion of the evidence of an Ophirian origin which might have brought men to the New World in 1943 B.C. He did not explain the connection of Issachar with the Ophirites, and seemed to be offering an alternative to the Issachar origin. Apparently he was not committed to Issachar, but merely thought it most probable.

Vazquez (1948:22–23) also admitted other possible sources for the

Indians: Jews fleeing from Sennacherib about 700 B.C. through West
Africa and thence to America; Carthaginians, Scandinavians, Tatars,·
Chinese. Nonetheless, he remained convinced that "the most reasonable theory seems to be that they are descended from the Ten Tribes"
—especially the tribe of Issachar (1948:23). This descent was indicated by many of the "customs, rites, and ceremonies" common to the
ancient Hebrews and modern Indians. The examples which Vazquez
(1948:23–28) introduced were typical: similarity in physique and
temperament, circumcision, burial customs, language, et al. He did not
place much faith in the presumed equivalence of "Peru" and "Ophir,"
nor did he think the easy metamorphosis of "Indio" into "Iudio" by
inverting the "n" carried any significance. The multiplicity of languages, which Vazquez (1948:27–35) placed at fifty thousand, was a
problem to any theory of a common origin for the Indians, but Vazquez passed the diversity off as a consequence of sin or diabolic inter-
vention.

Despite the Jewish descent of the Indians, their remoteness from the
Old World freed them from any guilt in the death of Christ, and their
ready acceptance of Christianity from the Spaniards argued well for
them. "Although they were once idolaters," Vazquez (1948:34) argued, "we must judge them as one of the noblest peoples on earth."
This conclusion seems inconsistent with an adherence to the Issachar
variant of the Lost Tribes theory, but Vazquez gave no evidence of
concern over a possible inconsistency.

The only other writer this author found who accepted the Issachar
variation of the Ten Lost Tribes theory was Balthassar de Medina in
his *Chrónica de la Santa Provincia de San Diego de México* of 1682.
Although Medina (1682:fol. 223*v*) thought the South Americans and
Yucatecans were descendants of the gentile Iectan (father of Ophir),
"the Mexicans are originally of the ten tribes captured by Salmanazar,"
and of the family of Issachar, "whom the Indians recognized as their
special ancestor."

García did not consider all the possible theories available to Spanish
scholars after 1607. The *Origen* contained most of them, but post-
Garcían writers added many variations unfamiliar to García. García
himself contributed a variation to the theory which received the most

extensive elaboration in the seventeenth century: that the earliest inhabitants of America descended from peoples from the Iberian peninsula. Oviedo suggested the earliest version of this theory in 1535 with the Hesperian story (1944–1945:I, 46). López de Gómara (1941:I, 115) advanced a variant reading of the Spanish theory in 1552 when he rejected the settlement of America by Spaniards fleeing the Moors after the defeat of King Rodrigo in 711. García repeated the former two versions with considerable supporting comment, and added a Spanish migration in Roman times (1729:173–187).

Solórzano (1703:10) repeated the Moorish variation of the Spanish-origin theory in 1629, having found the story both in López de Gómara and in Juan de Mariana's very popular *Historia general de España* (Toledo, 1592), but he did not accept this theory. Mariana's *Historia* went through fifteen impressions before 1780; it included another variation of the Iberian origin theory. This, the fourth Spanish-origin theory, claimed that the descendants of Tubal—mythical progenitor of the early Iberians—settled the Indies (Solórzano, 1703: 11). Calancha, as he did with most other theories, curtly dismissed the various Spanish-Indian ideas (1638:41).

The second book dealing exclusively with the origins of the American Indians, written by a Spaniard and published in his lifetime, appeared in Lima in 1681: *Tratado único y singular del origen de los indios del Perú, Méjico, Santa Fé y Chile*, by Diego Andrés Rocha, a judge of the Audiencia of Lima. In this book Rocha proposed "that the Americans take their origin from the primitive inhabitants of Spain in the first place, and from the Israelites, and Tartars in the second" (1891:I, xi).

Rocha paid tribute to García by copying his essay on the four ways of knowing. He did refine it somewhat by identifying *Fé Humana* as "Tradition," which made it more meaningful than in García's writing. But he still concluded, as had García, that only *Opinión* could apply to the search for Indian origins (1891:I, 18–19). Rocha freely admitted the inability of the "opinion method" to give verifiable results.

Rocha briefly sketched the various theories of Indian origins. He borrowed freely from García, but he also added much that had come to light since 1607. He noted that Torquemada, Solórzano, and Calancha had referred to the Carthaginian theory, and that Solórzano had commented on the Phoenician origin. In each case he left the impression that those writers supported the ideas that he mentioned. They did not (1891:I, 19–26). Rocha continued in similar vein through a discussion of theories of origins from Tatars, Atlanteans, Ophirians, and Courlanders (1891:I, 26–43).

After this background, Rocha introduced his reasons for adhering to an initial Spanish (i.e., Basque) settlement. He claimed to believe:

that these West Indies, after the Universal Flood, began to be populated by the descendants of Japheth, son of Noah. From Japheth descended Tubal, who settled Spain . . . (with) his descendants . . . and these, as they were neighbors to the Isla Atlántida, came as settlers by way of it and arrived at Tierra Firme . . . (1891:I, 47–49)

and inhabited every land from the Straits of Magellan to the Straits of Anian. Reason, and "the nearness of the continent of Cádiz [Atlantis] to Cartagena [in Colombia] of these Indies," suggest the Iberians as the earliest migrants to America.

Reason did not stand alone. It drew support from the numerous similarities between the Indians and the ancient inhabitants of Spain. These ancient Spaniards shared an aptitude for war with the Araucanos and the Caribs. The dominant timidity of the Indian population resulted from migrations subsequent to the coming of the Basques to America (1891:I, 49–55). The ancient Iberians lived in a wild state and ate and slept under the stars; so did many of the Indians. Both peoples tended to idolatry and barbarity, and both were simple, short, and heavy-set. Both practiced human sacrifice; their festivals and flutes were similar. They both wore two braids; the men underwent sympathetic labor pains, and the women took care of them; both labored in the field; and neither used money. Both possessed rude customs, and wore the poncho-type overcloak; both peoples killed their children to prevent their enslavement, and both lived on wild fruits. Both nations lived in small, separated groups, and neither loved the pursuit of "science" (1891:I, 55–67). In addition, the Iberians and Indians used similar weapons and had similar customs in the conduct of war. These weapons included the lance, the short sword, bow and arrow, poisoned arrows, war paint and war apparel, smoke signals, and female soldiers (1891:I, 68–74).

Rocha also argued that the Indian languages possessed several words in common with the most ancient Spanish language, Vizcaíno (Basque). The Vizcaínos had retained most of the original language of Tubal while other Spaniards mixed theirs with foreign languages. Furthermore, the Basques experienced far less trouble in learning Quechua, because of their linguistic affinities with the Incas—an affinity resulting from the fact that the Indians had come tó America some four thousand years ago when Tubal's language still predominated in Iberia (1891:I, 73–78). Then Rocha listed several words common to the Quechua and the Basque languages (1891:I, 79–80):

salt: *gache* or *gacha* in Basque, and *cache* in Quechua
water: *vura* (B); *jurac* (Q) meant white, i.e., the imitation of water
cask: *upia* (B); *upiai* (Q) meant "to drink"
the ceremonial kiss: *mucho* (B) ; *muchar* or *mochar* (Q)

Similarities in the names of geographical features abounded. The old name for America, *Anaguac,* i.e., "ana" and "gua," meant "surrounded by water." The names of many of the rivers of Spain began with "gua" such as Guadalquivir and Guadiana. Only in Spain and America could one find villages and rivers whose names began with the prefix "gua." But America possessed such villages and towns as Guaxaca [Oaxaca], Guatemala, Guánaco [Huánaco in Peru], Guano, Guayaquil, Guancabélica [Huancavélica], and dozens more (1891:I, 80–82).

Rocha reported that the Indians had, in olden times, used the name "Andes" as the name for all of America; they borrowed that word from Spain (1891:I, 83). The inhabitants of Florida had named their village Tobal after their ancestral progenitor Tubal. The natives of Cuba honored Tubal's brother, Javan, by naming the city of Havana for him. Tubal's nephew, Iectan, had lent his name to Yucatán. The primitive name of Spain, "Pania," now applied to Paria in Venezuela. Similar comparisons filled several more pages, but Rocha did reject one. He thought that the Spaniards may have named the village of

Salamanca near Arequipa, because he could not trace the name back beyond 1550 (1891:I, 83–90).

"Who cannot see the conformity which Libichuca of this America has with Libisuca or Libisoca of primitive Spain?" Or Guayaquil with Guarte Araquil in ancient Aragon (1891:I, 92, 95)? Numerous similarities in personal names also showed up. "Paulo," from the Inca "Paullu," came to America from Rome, probably brought by the Carthaginians whom Rocha planned to introduce later in his account (1891: I, 105, 123–125).

Rocha then returned to cultural traits common to both Indians and ancient Spaniards. He noted the use of vermillion to paint the face, excessive drinking, use of leather barques, polygamy, illiteracy, lack of knowledge of or cultivation of wheat (earlier he had claimed the early Spaniards made a drink called *cesía* or *cería* from "trigo y cebada y otras raíces"), melancholy, Flood traditions, and indifference to gold and silver (1891:I, 109–130).

At the conclusion of this extensive catalogue of similarities supporting his thesis, Rocha restated it on more narrowly geographic grounds. Although, he wrote (1891:I, 133–136), Norway and parts of Africa lay closer to the Indies than Spain at the present time, in the old days people from Spain could more readily get to the New World because of the island of Atlantis which began at Cádiz and reached to the vicinity of Mexico; Greenland lay thousands of miles farther away than Atlantis.

It seems that Rocha had a reason other than curiosity for discovering the origins of the Indians.

After the Deluge Spaniards went to the New World, and after many centuries God restored it to Spain by right of reversion. . . . Oh, the profundity of the wisdom and science of the Most High who after so many centuries ordained that these islands be restored to the Crown of Spain by Columbus (1891:I, 137).

Not only did Spain possess the reversionary interests of the ancient Iberians, but since the Spanish royal family had Gothic blood, and Rocha (1891:I, 138–140) intended to prove that the Gothic Scythians also came to America, Spain could, therefore, claim the Scythian reversion.

From time to time Rocha had pointed out certain weaknesses in the character of the Indians which could not have been inherited from the ancient Spaniards. The source of these weaknesses lay in the character of the late-comers to America who had mixed to a certain extent with the earlier settlers: "I am certain that many of the West Indians descended from the ten tribes which Shalmaneser carried into exile, and who came as settlers to the coasts of Mexico by way of the kingdom of Anian" (1891:I, 154–155). However, this influence was introduced after the Spanish, and such Spain-based settlers as the Carthaginians, had populated the area.

Rocha added very little to the Ten Lost Tribes theory other than to make it a secondary source of the American population. He took the traditional Esdras-based version and brought the Jews to America where they mixed somewhat with the original settlers, thus producing the weaknesses in character evident in some Indians. After the restoration by Columbus, the Spaniards rescued the Jews of the Lost Tribes by making them Catholics (1891:I, 155–164). Then followed a long catalogue of similarities between Jews and Indians. On occasion Rocha duplicated an argument he had used earlier to illustrate a Spanish descent. For example, he referred to Yucatán as a Jewish word (1891:I, 204); he compared Jewish with Indian hair styles [no longer in braids] and cloaks (1891:I, 217); he found also that the Quechua language [previously Basque] greatly resembled Hebrew (1891:I, 218–219).

Rocha took much of his material from García, but in one instance he borrowed from Calancha a story which Calancha considered ridiculous: Another proof "that the Hebrews and Americans are of one origin is to see that this word *Indio* with the *n* inverted says *Iudio,* and this transformation is very simple" (1891:II, 35).

Rocha spent sixty pages tracing the route of the Jews to America and concluded, as he had already stated, that they came via Anian. Their travels took them from Assyria and the cities of the Medes through Persia, Scythia, and Tatary to Anian and finally Mexico. En route they picked up several identifiable Old World customs and seventy-one place names which they later applied to America (1891:II, 86–96): They acquired also some stray peoples, such as the Tatars [Scythians] and brought them to America (1891:II, 86, 97–101).

Finally, Rocha met the objections to his theoretical construct. How did he account for the differences in the color of the brown Indians and the white Spaniards and Jews? He replied that climate and other associated factors caused the color of the skin to change. These factors had not caused the modern Spaniards to change, because such an alteration required several generations uninfluenced by new blood from outside the region (1891:II, 107–111).

He explained the lack of beards in a similar fashion. Climatic variations and "the accidents of the signs and the planets" could act upon hair which appeared after birth and cause people to lose it (1891:II, 111–116). He replied to the other objections—the failure of the Jewish Indians to keep their laws, the lack of writing, and the vagueness and uncertainty of Esdras—in the standard Garcían manner (1891:II, 116–137).

The most striking characteristic of Rocha's *Tratado único y singular* was that it contained little that García could not have included in the *Origen;* and, indeed, little that he had not. Rocha did cite authorities who had written after 1607, but he did not always cite them accurately. Furthermore, he included little genuinely new material, but mainly material that had been restated since 1607. He gives the impression that he could have, and probably did, write his book with García's *Origen de los indios* as his major source. Rocha, in essence, took the sections on Spain and the Lost Tribes from García, elaborated on them somewhat, meshed them together into a "new" theory, and sprinkled the result with a few Carthaginians and Tatars.

Rocha did a disservice to such men as Solórzano, Torquemada, and Calancha when he quoted them erroneously to support his construction. Their thinking was far in advance of his, and doubtless they would have laughed at his theory just as they laughed at most others. They at least approached their subject with some degree of skepticism and a critical consideration of methodology. None of them borrowed García's four-method scheme.

Most commentators contented themselves with attempting to discover the origins of the first Americans after the Deluge. Three—Simón (1627), Calancha (1638), and Augustín de Vetancurt (1698)— made more or less detailed investigations into the possibility of antediluvian man in America. Simón thought that the fact that God made man to rule over and people the Earth indicated that people had come to the New World before the Flood. He knew of some evidence pointing in that direction. For example, some Peruvians reported finding a ship high in the Andes, no doubt carried there by the Flood. He also had reports of elephant bones found in Mexico; since elephants did not now live in Mexico, they must have lived there before the Deluge. He had heard too of the discovery of the bones of giants in both Mexico and Peru; and all giants had drowned in the Flood (1627:30–32).

Simón still had to explain how men and animals got to America even if they did come before the Flood. He suggested that perhaps the Old World had been geographically continuous with the New, before Noah. Even without such contiguity, Adam probably knew enough "science" to tell his descendants how to get to America by ship (1627: 32–33). Augustín de Vetancurt followed Simón very closely in his *Teatro mexicano* (1698: pt. 2, fol. 2), and added nothing to the earlier account. Calancha (1638:35–36) likewise followed Simon very closely. He did, however, write a much clearer statement.

The location of Paradise played a small part in the debate over Indian origins in the seventeenth century. No one claimed that the present Indians originated in the New World because the Garden of Eden was there. The common belief placed Paradise in Mesopotamia, and most people thought that the Ark had landed in Armenia. To locate Paradise in the New World would not solve the question of the origins of America's current inhabitants. But a few Europeans wondered if perhaps Adam and Eve might have lived in America.

Solórzano (1703:6) pondered that possibility, but decided that he could not give an answer. He thought that even if Paradise were not in the New World, its perpetual spring and favorable climate deserved all the praise the ancients lavished on the Elysian Fields and the Fortunate Isles. The *Isagoge* (1935:41–48) went much further and argued that America probably was the site of Paradise.

The great Spanish bibliographer Antonio León Pinelo wrote a substantial manuscript developing the idea of *El Paraíso en el Nuevo Mundo,* which he completed in 1656, fifty-five years before the *Isagoge.* A massive study, finally published in two volumes in 1943, it contained over a quarter of a million words. After a long introductory section citing the numerous reasons for placing the original home of man in the New World, León Pinelo explained that although the Ark landed in Armenia, it had set out on its voyage from America (1943: I, 284).

The author went on to explain that the sins of Noah's contemporaries contaminated the Indies. That was why God caused Noah to land in Armenia. As a further consequence of this contamination, the Indies remained uninhabitable for several centuries. León Pinelo argued that "no man entered the Continent of the Indies . . . where we supposed Paradise to be, the habitation of Adam, and of his first descendents," until the time of Christ. The death of Christ lifted the contamination of the Indies, redeeming Paradise as well as man (1943:I, 286–287).

León Pinelo accepted a delayed version of the Ten Lost Tribes thesis to account for the first postdiluvian immigration. In effect, he used the traditional account, changing only the time of arrival.

Spanish writers after García seldom followed him on the question how the problems posed by the Indians' presence in America could be solved. Rocha, in his *Tratado único y singular,* accepted García's methodological assumptions without question. Vetancurt (1698: pt. 2, fol. 2–10) showed a similar debt to García. His review of the various theories and his discussion of the four ways of knowing came from the *Origen* with only slight changes. Vetancurt also adopted as his own the all-embracing conclusion of the *Origen.*

Torquemada (1613), Simón (1627), Solórzano (1629), and Calancha (1638) did not even refer to the four-method system, though all of them knew of García's book. They did not always understand it. Solórzano (1703:9) wrote of the *Origen de los indios,* "where after having labored hard in documenting and supporting twelve different opinions, he came to reject them, and resolve that none of them could be admitted, and left the subject in great doubt." Had Solórzano read a little further he would have discovered an acceptance as well as a rejection of the various theories.

Two major themes dominated the considerations of how one could discover the origins of the Indians: the presence of animals, and the legitimacy of cultural comparisons. Torquemada worried at length about the animals. America seemed to be an island, and while Torquemada conceded that men could have come by ship, and the birds could fly over, but what of the animals—especially the *animales bravos?* Did an angel bring them? Perhaps; but he tended to agree with Acosta that the animals, and presumably the men too, probably came by land (1723:I, 21–22, 29; Villagutierre, 1701:27–28).

Pedro Simón did not concur. He thought that the Carthaginians might have brought the animals with them in their ships for sporting purposes. Despite that possibility, Simón did not know for certain that the Carthaginians came to America. Issachar, his favorite candidate for progenitor of the Indians, apparently came by land (1627:33–36, 37–43).

The question surrounding the arrival of animals in the New World also played an important part in Solórzano's considerations. He did not believe that they could all have come by ship. Drawing from Acosta, he suggested that in some as yet unexplored area, America came near enough to the Old World for animals and men to pass over easily (1703:10–11). The Chilean, Alonso de Ovalle, in his *Histórica relación del Reyno de Chile* of 1646, came to a similar conclusion, virtually adopting Acosta's position as his own (1646:79–82).

Torquemada, Solórzano, Simón, and Calancha also seriously questioned the technique of discovering relationships between peoples separated by space and time. Torquemada not only denied the presence of Hebraic languages in America but suggested that the comparison of languages could not indicate origins. Moreover, he disputed the value of comparing customs (1723:I, 26–27). In this latter case Torquemada objected to a particular application and not necessarily to the technique as such. It failed in this case because most "Jewish" customs were not peculiarly Jewish, and Gentiles had adopted all the bad customs of the Hebrews (1723:I, 26–27). Torquemada also argued that comparisons did not produce definite proof. Furthermore, many comparisons made in the past were erroneous (1723:I, 27).

Not all Indians possessed the same characteristics, Torquemada argued. Many were not liars, or superstitious, or any of the other things they were called (1723:I, 27). This posed some different questions. Did the Indians possess a core of cultural traits common to all? Would the comparative technique be valid even in that case? Did those who disputed the application of the technique to America intend a general rejection?

Pedro Simón insisted that the Indians did have several traits in common in pre-Columbian times (1627:10–11). These included cannibalism, sodomy, nudity, shamelessness, cold-bloodedness, ingratitude, drunkenness, viciousness, fickleness, cruelty, vindictiveness, irreligion, thievery, mendacity, adultery, a love of novelties, and a lack of reverence for the aged. Simón did not generalize from this and accept the validity of the comparative technique. He merely wanted to prove that the Indians did have a common origin.

That origin must be determined by "conjecture and good reason, without the aid of authentic writing." Any theory must of necessity conform to the Catholic faith on the point of the descent of all men from Adam through Noah, for "we cannot with temerity affirm that God created these men anew" (1627:34). Simón's own method did not employ specific trait comparisons. He based his belief that the Americans descended from Issachar on a juxtaposition of the general status of the Indians against the status prophesied for Issachar's descendants (1627:36–43).

Calancha completely rejected Simón's technique. The condition of servitude of a people could not indicate their origin, he maintained (1638:37, 40), because serfs and other inferior peoples existed everywhere—even in Spain. The conditions Simón described, he added, could fit various peoples, such as Christians living in Moorish lands and Negroes in Europe. Calancha also rejected the argument that the Indians must have descended from Ham because of the curse and the servitude of the Indians. He thought that line of reasoning absurd, since Canaan, not Ham, drew the curse, and the method proved nothing (1638:36–37).

Solórzano devoted more consideration to matters of method than did Torquemada, Simón, or Calancha. The problem—

from whom the Southern and Western Indians descended, and how such people found all the Islands, and Tierra Firme of the New World is with reason cast in doubt. And when, how, and from where could they have passed to them, seeing as how they are separated from the rest of the world by all the ocean, and that they were apparently unknown to the Ancients (1703:9)?

In finding the answers to these questions we should not "ask what God could have done," but how we can understand what He did, according to the order of things, and human reason (1703:9).

Reason dictated that the natives of America had to come to the New World after the Flood. To maintain that they survived the Deluge would be repugnant to Scripture. Nor would it be legitimate to hold that "the first people of these Provinces were engendered from the soil, or from some putrefaction of it aided by the heat of the sun," because only imperfect animals such as flies, frogs, or rats could be produced in such a fashion. The "impious and heretical opinion of Amado de Villa-Nueva . . . who affirms that a true man can be formed by the chemical art" was likewise unacceptable. Finally, one could not "create or form [a man] by black magic, nor from the union" of various species of animals (1703:9–10).

How then did men get to America? Torquemada and Solórzano felt that they must seek a land route, by virtue of the fact that America lay far from the centers of the ancient world and the ancients did not know of it; but they must also seek a land route because it alone could account for the *animales bravos*. Calancha came to the same conclusion from largely geographical considerations. He knew from the *Relación* of the voyage of the Nodal brothers, published in 1621, that recent exploration of the southern tip of South America indicated that South America did not approach any other land mass. Calancha proposed, then, that since it seemed unlikely the first settlers could have crossed the Atlantic or Pacific, they must have come by a land route; and that route must lie in the North. He thought that northwestern America was the most likely place for such a route (1638:42).

Calancha asserted that the first Americans probably descended from the Tatars, who in turn descended from the gentile Japheth. The Tatars seemed the best candidates simply because they inhabited the region nearest the Strait of Anian (1638:42–43). He also conceded the possibility that northeastern America joined, or came near, Europe. If so, some Lapps or Courlanders might have come to the New World by that route. But those peoples also descended from Tatars (1638:42–43): "I am certain that when the Flood passed and the sea returned to its bed, and the water to its basements, it was all one continuous land, without any Strait, from Tartary to Chile." This had to be the case or the animals could not have come to the Indies.

Calancha did not reason solely from geography and fauna. He thought that the similarities of the Tatars and Indians indicated that they were the same people. He mentioned many cultural similarities— customs, habits, religion—but others were physical, such as color and appearance (1638:42, 44). Earlier, Calancha had disputed the validity of using color as a measure of origins because the Indians lacked a common color (1638:37). In the end he had to adopt the use of color and the "one reason (which in all nations and ages has been authentic proof) whereby relationships could be indicated": comparison of color, customs, religion, and conditions (1638:44).

Torquemada and Solórzano did not come out so strongly for the Tatar origin theory. Torquemada (1723:I, 29) apparently leaned toward it, but he did not commit himself to any theory. Solórzano wrote that:

our Indians in most certainty originated in most part in the East, or . . . China or Tartary: thus Arias Montano called them Ophirites, thinking they descended from Iectan, Ophir, and Hevilay, who were the populators of the East. In truth there is much similarity between the two Indias, in . . . conditions, rites, customs, and especially in their color. . . .(1703:11).

The Mexican-Spaniard Alonso de Benavides added some support to the Tatar-Chinese tradition in his revised *Memoria* of 1634. He reported that the Indians of the Mexican coast had an old legend of descent from the Chinese (1945:39–40).

A review of the thinking of the four major Spanish commentators of the early seventeenth century is instructive. Torquemada denied the validity of the comparative technique. Consequently, though he concluded from geography and the fauna of America that a land connection probably existed in the North, he could not find a basis for advancing a personal theory of Indian origins. Simón, the least advanced of the four, used a strictly exegetical technique. He based his theory in toto on biblical tradition and ancient references.

Solórzano made an extensive study of the problem how to discover the Indians' origins. He eliminated miracles, but he did not contest the legitimacy of cultural comparisons. Geographical and faunal considerations led him, as they had Torquemada, to the North in search of a land route. Unlike Torquemada, who in effect rejected the possibility of determining origins, Solórzano argued that the Tatars, or other Far Eastern peoples, must have migrated into America and produced the Indians. Although Calancha's arguments were developed to greater lengths, his conclusions conformed with those of Solórzano. Another writer of the period, Andrés Pérez de Ribas (1645:19), was content to state, in his *Historia de los triumphos de nuestra santa fee entre gentes las más bárbaras, y fieras del nuevo Orbe* of 1645, that "the most probable opinion . . . says they came by land continent with Asia in the north part, or [separated] by some narrow arm of the sea, which was easy for them to pass, and which is as yet undiscovered."

Torquemada (1613), Solórzano (1629), and Calancha (1638), relying to a great extent on Acosta (1589/1590) and Herrera (1601/1613), were the champions of the Acostan Tradition in early seventeenth-century Spain. By 1638 they had pushed the accepted methodology to its limits again and again. With no help from non-Spanish scholars these five men had reached the conclusion which twentieth century science would someday substantiate. Their deliberations led them to consider factors such as the geographical situation of America with respect to the Old World and the lack of convincing evidence that the ancients knew of the New World. In addition, when the problem of the origin of man in the New World was united with the equally perplexing problem of the origins of American animals, these scholars were drawn to the inescapable conclusion that America *must* be connected somewhere to the Old World. A land bridge *must* exist now, or must have existed in the past. The most logical explanation was now apparent: that the separation of the Old and New worlds must be so narrow that migration was possible.

But where could one go after reaching this position? They could say with some certainty how the Americans must have come to the New World. They believed also that America probably was settled in regular and continuing fashion as a consequence of the expansion of the human race. But they could not conclusively determine whether the Indians derived from the Tatars, who lived closest to America, or whether they came to the New World in a special migration of the Jews through Tatary.

A comparison of cultural traits could not indicate to everyone's satisfaction that the Indians more closely resembled the Tatars than the Hebrews of the Ten Lost Tribes. To Acosta the comparative technique seemed useless because the Indians probably developed their own culture after arriving in America. Herrera and Torquemada did not go quite that far; but they were sufficiently conscious of the weakness of the comparative technique to avoid committing themselves to any opinion. Solórzano and Calancha used the technique to identify the Indians as Tatars; but they used it sparingly.

One difficulty in the way of new methodological developments was the failure to recognize that populations might derive their cultures from one source and their physique from another. The writers of the age did not conceive the question in biological terms. Commentators had, it is true, noted such physical factors as color, hair, and facial features; but they attached no great importance to them. The belief that climatic conditions could alter physical appearances hindered the development of physical criteria. Hair was the physical characteristic most frequently noted; but commentators argued primarily over its absence or presence, or about the style in which the native wore it.

Though Acosta's influence dominated the major writers from 1613 to 1638, it scarcely shows in the published literature after 1638. But a manuscript by a fellow-Jesuit in 1653 does reveal considerable concern with the problem of the discoverability of Indian origins. Bernabé Cobo, whose *Historia del Nuevo Mundo* did not appear in print until 1890–1893, spent more than fifty years in the Indies. With such experience, he was in a better position than most writers to comment on the character of the Indians, and whether there was a core of customs common to all the natives.

Cobo had several doubts about the common origin of the Indians. The natives, he pointed out, did not have a name for all America which all recognized; nor did they have a common name for all the peoples of the New World. Even the Peruvians had no name for *all* the people of their empire; the closest thing to it was the Quechua word "Runa" which meant "man" (1890–1893:I, 107; III, 11–12). Despite this important objection, Cobo still thought the Indians all came from the same stock. He based this opinion largely on a belief that the Indians did possess certain traits in common (1890–1893:III, 36–38). But beyond the cultural similarities, Cobo argued that the physical similarities of the Indians were also of great importance. They all had the same color—somewhat brown. This color varied some, but not to a significant degree. And, he added, concerning the varieties of colors in the world,

I am convinced that this variety of colors is not caused by the climate where one is born, but that it is a part of men and that we take it from nature, despite the fact that we all came originally from Adam and Eve; and that God ordained it thus for the beauty of the Universe and to show his infinite wisdom and omnipotence in this diversity of colors (1890–1893:III, 13–14).

Cobo noted other physical characteristics such as the stature and corpulence of the Indians. Since these did not vary much, he thought this indicative of a common origin (1890–1893:III, 17). Cobo found even greater uniformity in the eyes of the Indians. All Indians had black eyes; none had green or blue ones. He also pointed out the distinctive almond shape of the eyes and noted that it was caused by the eyelids. So distinctive was this particular characteristic that to tell if a person were a mestizo "we look them in the eyes" and there can be no doubt, because the corners of the eyes reflect the degree of Indian blood (1890–1893:III, 18).

Cobo also noted that hair had physical characteristics in addition to its mere presence or absence. All Indians had black hair; it was never blond, rarely absent from the head, and seldom greyed. Moreover, the texture of Indian hair was very coarse (1890–1893:III, 18–19).

The combination of physical and cultural characteristics common to all Indians convinced Cobo that "it was doubtless one nation or family of men which passed to people this land" (1890–1893:III, 48–49). The biggest objection to this theory lay in "the incredible multitude of languages" (Cobo estimated more than two thousand) used by the Indians. But this very variety provided an answer. If each language represented a separate migration, why did no one know how they came to America? Where could two thousand nations come from? And why should two thousand peoples preserve languages as their only major distinction (1890–1893:III, 49–50)?

Cobo argued that one language could differentiate into two thousand, just as the old Roman language had given rise to many languages. Without writing to stabilize speech, primitive languages probably changed much faster. He found evidence for such an argument in a comparison of the Quechua and Aymara languages of Peru, which he thought developed from the same parent language (1890–1893: III, 50–53). Cobo did not seem to wonder why languages should change with no similar changes in other aspects of culture.

The solution to the problem of origins offered by Cobo came largely from Solórzano. On several occasions (as when writing "we are not investigating what God could do . . . ," but how it could be done in the course of human affairs) Cobo's language closely paralleled Solórzano's. His conclusion that the Indians came from East Asia also came from Solórzano (1890–1893:III, 63–66). He did, however, offer a few elaborations and one important demurrer. Cobo did not think that there was any connection between the migration of men and the migration of animals. Evidence of this lack of connection was that all domestic animals in the New World were native to it; i.e., the immigrants had not brought their Old World domestic animals with them (1890–1893:III, 67–76). Why did the Indians bring no animals with them? The point is unclear in Cobo's work, but he seems to have thought the Indians came to America soon after the Flood, before they possessed cattle.

Cobo fell distinctly in the Acostan Tradition, and he carried the ar-

guments begun by Acosta to new heights, even though he abandoned
the animal-migration phase of it. The unfortunate circumstances which
prevented the publication of his work greatly impeded the development of Spanish and foreign scholarship on the subject of the origins
of the American Indians. Not only did Cobo advance the best tradition
in Spanish scholarship; but he came close to formulating the new criteria necessary to the clarification and continued development of that
tradition.

Cobo's remarks on the peculiar physical properties of the Indians
were not offered as an alternative to the cultural comparison technique.
He continued to rely on that method for determining the relationship
of Indians to Old World peoples. But publication of these remarks
might well have led to a wider application of physical, as opposed to
cultural, comparisons. The problems which Acosta thought impossible
under the old investigative procedure might have yielded to this new
method sufficiently to encourage its development. Under those circumstances, the distinction between physical and cultural origins which began to crop up in Northern literature in the late seventeenth century
might have entered Spanish literature too.

Unfortunately, Cobo's *History* was not published. Few writers after
Calancha (1638) showed the Acostan influence. Without the new di-
rections which Cobo's work could have supplied, the tradition stagnated in Spain. The only important restatements of the tradition after
1638 came with the republication of Solórzano in 1703, and Torquemada in 1723.

Several factors mitigated against the success of the Acostan Tradition, and reveal Rocha's *Tratado único y singular* of 1681 and the revived and expanded *Origen de los indios* of 1729 as less anachronistic
than the previous pages might indicate. The recent historical experience of Spain itself constituted a strong argument for a trans-Atlantic
migration. A pre-Columbian migration seemed not so unreasonable
when viewed against the vast numbers of Europeans who had gone to
America since 1492. Why then deny that the Carthaginians could have
gone? Or the Greeks? Or the Romans? Or the ancient Spaniards themselves?

The absence of any historical record of such an event did not prove it had not happened. Knowledge, as the Renaissance knew so well, could easily be mislaid. Furthermore, ancient literature contained many veiled hints and allusions to legends of Atlantic lands which might refer to the New World.

Other factors retarding the success of the Acostan school were the inability of the writers to find a substitute for the accepted methodology and the failure of Europeans in general to identify degrees of reliability and authority. García and Rocha were ultimately as unable to give definite answers as Acosta. They openly advised their readers that certainty would not be achieved in the field of Indian origins. Since they could offer only opinions which one could accept or not, by implication they invited disbelief. García, of course, went so far as to proclaim that all opinions on the subject, except the Indians', possessed equal probability.

García, trapped by his intellectual assumptions, genuinely believed all theories probable. Rocha, trapped by a nationalistic spirit, believed he had discovered the *most* probable one even though it depended on the prior existence of the generally discredited Atlantis. A question arises then: Did the second edition of the *Origen de los indios* in 1729 show any development away from or advance over the 1607 version?

In the late 1720's Andrés Gonzalez de Barcia Carballido y Zúñiga looked over the books on the subject of the origins of the American Indians. He considered those which treated the subject either by design or in passing and found García's the best. He, then,

decided to reprint it, adding . . . other opinions that were not hidden from the notice of Fr. Gregorio, although he did not stop to mention them; and mentioning in the margin or in the text whatever came to our attention during the printing . . . We change or contradict nothing in what we add or declare: we point out the additions in the text between two brackets [ ] (García, 1729: "proemio").

García had not referred to very many authorities; editor Barcia added hundreds of marginal bibliographical notes. Many of them referred to materials available in 1607, but most referred to works printed since that time which in any way bore on the subject of Indian origins.

Barcia's major contributions to the *Origen de los indios* consisted of

voluminous insertions into the text itself. Sometimes the printer omit-
ted the brackets, but the nature of the added part and the style usually
identified it. True to his promise in the "Proemio" Barcia added nothing contradictory. His additions took the form of extensions to García's
catalogues of evidences; some of these additions ran more than twenty
pages. A few of the expansions referred to opinions not available to
García. One, in particular, concerned the supposed equation of St.
Brandon Isle (ca. 560 A.D.) with the Indies (1729:32–33). Another
major addition elaborated on the possibility of Phoenician settlement,
unimportant in García's own time. Barcia inserted thirty-eight pages of
"proofs" of this theory (1729:196–239).

At the end of the volume Barcia added a long section on new theories derived largely from non-Spanish sources. He attributed an Egyptian origin theory to Athanasius Kircher (1729:248–254); Barcia distinguished separate African and Ethiopian origins (1729:254–259)
and mentioned Simón's Issachar and Martín's Courlanders (1729:
256–257; 262–263); and he catalogued supposed origins from
France, Cambria and Ireland, Troy, Norway and Denmark, Frisia, and
Scythia (1729:259–262; 263–273; 289–303). In each case Barcia followed the first author's practice of stating and meeting all objections,
leaving each of the thirteen new possibilities uncontested. Even the
most inconsequential theory—the derivation of the Chileans from the
Frisian islands off the coast of Greenland or Iceland because "Chile"
meant "frío," which obviously derived from Frisia—received this type
of endorsement.

Barcia had not read widely in non-Spanish literature. Most of his
information came from the Dutch Georg Horn whose *De Originibus
Americanis* appeared in editions of 1652 and 1669. Barcia made no
secret of his dislike for the Protestant Horn, but he accepted his arguments.

Barcia also added a little to the first author's discussion concerning
knowledge through *Opinión*.

To obtain the origin one must base it in Language, Customs, Religion, and
conformity of names, and words, and even of the features and hair style,
and adornment. . . . Horn affirmed that conformity argued one origin of

the peoples, and disconformities different origins. . . . To avoid these errors it is necessary to have other specifics in addition to the conformity of the name (of peoples) . . . to legitimatize the conjectures. It is not sufficient to have a few words that agree in meaning and sound to establish Opinion, but many, special ones. Nor is the diversity of languages enough to distinguish between nations: the Chinese and Japanese have very different languages and are one people. The same goes for the Mexicans and Tarascans, and even the Castillians and Basques. Nor can a comparison of two nations on the basis of what is common to many—such as the use of bows and arrows, lunar months, and the practice of living scattered in the hills which by themselves throw no light on the Origins—yield a conjecture which is not very weak (1729:11–12).

But, on the other hand, such things as arms, "insignias of the people," idols, sacrificial rites, mode of writing, and architectural style were very useful (1729:11–12).

In a certain sense Barcia's understanding of the usefulness of cultural comparisons showed a distinct advance over García. The editor recognized that the characteristics used must be of a peculiar rather than a general nature, an idea that can be traced to the very beginning of the debate, and that many writers, notably Las Casas and Acosta, recognized. García must have been aware that some had questioned the validity of cultural comparisons; but he did not listen to their restraining voices in the construction of his book. Barcia at least endorsed the limitation; but he did not always follow his endorsement. To García's original list of traits common to Indians and Carthaginians, Barcia added veneration of fire, use of skins for clothing, eating of dogs, use of signal fires, cruelty to captives, and mendacity (1729:50–52). None of these were anymore nearly peculiar to Indians and Carthaginians than were bows and arrows.

Barcia recognized that the comparative method had its limitations. But he had no means to determine what those limitations were. Apparently, he chose to ignore the problem in the editorial expansion of the *Origen*. The most remarkable characteristic of the revised *Origen* of 1729 is that García could have written it all in 1607 except for the references to later specific authors and theories. The addenda of 1729 did not vary from the earlier work in the form or content of the arguments. If the designations of the "Tatar" and "Scythian" opinions were switched, the change would not be readily discernible; for, given the confused state of the information on those two peoples (who were frequently thought of as one people) and given the nature of the "proofs" acceptable to García-Barcia, the supporting material *could* apply to either group.

At the beginning of this section this writer posed the question: Did the second edition of the *Origen de los indios* show any development away from or advance over the 1607 edition? The answer must be negative.

Indeed, the republication of the *Origen* in 1729 must be viewed as a distinctly regressive step. The finest products of Spanish scholarship on the subject of Indian origins were those I have designated the Acostan Tradition. The republication of the *Origen* reaffirmed the credulity of the Garcían Tradition and constituted an effective rejection of the Acostan school. The restraint and skepticism characteristic of the Acostan writers were alien to the structure and purpose of the *Origen*. The dozen "probable" origins of 1607 mushroomed into more than two dozen "probable" origins in 1729.

Between 1589 and 1638 the published members of the Acostan school—Acosta (1589–1590), Herrera (1601–1613), Torquemada (1631), Solórzano (1629–1646), and Calancha (1638)—had gradually eliminated trans-Atlantic origins and routes via the South Pacific. Geography and faunal distribution had convinced them that the first settlers must have come into the New World by way of the still undiscovered Straits of Anian.

Ten of Barcia's new "probabilities" came across the Atlantic.

CHAPTER IV

The Debate on the Origins of the
American Indians in Northern Europe

The Expansion of the Debate to Northern Europe, 1600–1640

SPANISH WRITERS dominated the development of ideas concerning the origins of the Indians of America until the beginning of the seventeenth century. After 1600 the peoples of northern Europe began to take a more active interest—especially the English and the Dutch. Most probably their interest in the origins of the natives of the Indies began with the discovery of the New World. They did not, however, contribute much to the literature on origins until the sixteenth century. Strangely enough, John Rastell, an Englishman, apparently phrased the question in print for the first time in his *Interlude of the Four Elements* of 1520:

> But in the Southe parte of that contrey,
> The people there go nakyd alway,
> The lande is of so great hete!
> And in the North parte all the clothes
> That they were is but bestes skynnes,
> They have no nother fete;
> But howe the people furst began
> In that contrey, or whens they cam,
> For clerkes it is a questyon (1848:31).

In the last eighty years of the century the British made no important contribution to the literature on Indian origins. Much the same held true for the French, the Dutch, and other northern Europeans. After 1600, Englishmen, Frenchmen, and Dutch began to go to the Indies in increasing numbers; and as their knowledge grew, their interest in the question of Indian origins likewise grew, making the origin problem an important one. For a generation or so, from about 1640 to 1675, controversies centering in Holland and Britain, but affecting all of northern Europe, influenced a few of the more important men in Europe. These arguments involved such different figures as Hugo Grotius and Oliver Cromwell. In that period dozens of academic dissertations on the subject of the American Indians appeared from the universities of northern Europe, for the topic became briefly a popular subject for doctoral candidates.

The Spanish scholars of the seventeenth century took little notice of developments outside Spain and her empire, apparently not realizing that the Northerners might have anything to offer. What little the Spanish writers did take from outside Spain came largely from the Frenchman Genebrard by way of García. The Latin treatises of Grotius, De Laet, and Horn were evidently unknown in Spain until the unfriendly references by editor Barcia in the 1729 *Origen*.

On the other hand, Northern scholars knew many of the Spanish authorities. Peter Martyr, Acosta, and a few others were known in English translations by 1604; they were also available in French. The first volume of Hakluyt, printed in 1589 and again in 1598–1600, contained many excerpts from Spanish authors. In 1613 and 1626 Samuel Purchas gave a brief review of Spanish authorities on the subject in his *Pilgrimage* and his *Pilgrimes* and published extensive excerpts on America from the works of Herrera, Acosta, Oviedo, López de Gómara, Schmidel, Garcilaso de la Vega, el Inca, Xérez, Pedro Sancho, Cabeza de Vaca, De Soto, and Las Casas. Several Latin "Cosmographia" were also available.

Until 1640 the northern European publications on the origins of the Indians were largely British. Most of the theories expounded in Spain found little acceptance in the North, and few Northerners showed any interest in a "Mediterranean" origin. John Smith (1808–1814:XIII,

2) knew of the Spanish claims of a Carthaginian origin, but he did not accept it in his *General History of Virginia* (London, 1624). Samuel Purchas (Pennington, 1966), who had read widely in Spanish literature, dismissed the Carthaginian theory and the use of Aristotle (if indeed Aristotle wrote the story, he observed) to show that America was "lately" inhabited: Purchas thought the ancients had no knowledge of the New World. The discovery of America, he said, was an "errour . . . more fortunate than learned" (1905–1906:I, 163, 74; 1613:609–610).

None of the Northerners of this period seemed to care much about the Atlantis origin theory. Purchas (1905–1906:I, 164) dismissed it as "allegoricall"; and Lescarbot, writing in 1609, thought it a myth (1907:I, 48–49). The theories of a Phoenician origin and the various Spanish origin theories found no adherents in Northern literature. Only Lescarbot (1907:I, 43) seemed to have known of the Spanish theories, and he merely referred to them in passing. One writer did, however, endorse a Mediterranean theory. The Englishman Thomas Morton in his *New English Canaan* (Amsterdam, 1637) thought the natives of New England "doe use very many words of both Greek and Latine, and to the same signification." He thought he could explain this by postulating a Trojan origin for the Indians, for Trojans would have a few Greek and Latin words (1947:15–18).

Northern scholars hardly noticed Ophir. Only Purchas gave it serious consideration. He knew of Arias Montanus' *Phaleg* and of his derivation of the name "Peru" from "Ophir," and "Yucatán" from "Iectan." Purchas, however, thought López de Gómara, Acosta, and Garcilaso de la Vega correctly attributed the word to a river, or to an Indian fisherman name "Beru" (1905–1906:I, 66–68). He continued:

Peru could not be Ophir if we conceive that Solomon brought thence Ivorie; and Peacockes. For Peacockes they read Parrots, and for Ivorie they are forced to take it up by the way in some place of Africa or India. . . . As for such . . . which think so huge and vast a tract of Land as that New World, might bee now empty of Elephants which then it had (for it is confessed by all Classike Authors, that America never saw Elephant) . . . why should not other kinds of Creatures bee uterly destroyed aswel as those, being more hurtful to the inhabitants . . .? But I deserve blame to fight with Elephants in America, which is with less than a shadow, and to lay siege to Castles in the Aire (1905–1906:I, 73–74).

The Ten Lost Tribes of Israel theory had surprisingly little influence on the early Northern scholars. The Frenchman Marc Lescarbot mentioned it in passing in his *History of New France,* published in French editions in 1609, 1611, and 1618 (1907:I, 43). Purchas (1905–1906:I, 159) dismissed the theory largely by implication, since he thought America "latlier peopled than the Apostles dayes." The other writers of the period mostly ignored the theory.

Lescarbot, in approaching the problem of Indian origins, noted that "some have made use of certain prophecies and revelations of Holy Scripture dragged in by the hair to prove, some that the Spaniards, others that the Jews should inhabit this new world. Others have thought that the inhabitants were a race of Ham, carried thither by the punishment of God when Joshua began his entry into the land of Canaan" (1907:I, 43–44). He thought this seemed confirmed by the fact that the Canaanites were cannibals, as were many Indians. Lescarbot (1907:I, 43–44) cited many other similarities, but he did not definitely commit himself to this Ham-Canaan theory.

The Canaanite theory received the support of William Strachey three years later. In his *History of Travell into Virginia Britania,* written about 1612 but not published until 1849, Strachey fully accepted that "it is very probable likewise that both in the travels and Idolatry of the famely of Cham, this portion of the World (west-ward from Africa upon the Atlantic Sea) became both peopled, and instructed in the forme of prophane worshippe" (1953:53–55). Strachey (1953:55) thought he had discovered sufficient similarities to substantiate his opinion, but one question did worry him:

But how the vagabond race of Cham might discend into this new world, without furniture (as may be questioned) of shipping and means to tempt the Seas, togither how this great Continent (divided from the other three) should become stoared with beasts, and some Fowle, of one and the same kynd with the other parts. . . .

He could not answer.

This same question had bothered Lescarbot. Shipwrecks might have furnished some people, provided there were women aboard ship. Lescarbot argued that women may well have gone on expeditions in ancient times. The reason they no longer went was that luxury had sapped the hardihood of both sexes. And, since he knew by experience that civilized men could resort to savagery if stranded, the trans-Atlantic route was possible (1907:I, 44–46). On the other hand, Lescarbot thought, Noah may have constructed a second Ark to bring settlers to America; he felt certain too that the ancients had visited the New World (1907:I, 47–49).

Still, he did not know how America had "become stoared with beasts." He borrowed, then, from Acosta and argued that all the continents either joined or came near to each other at such straits as Anian or Magellan. The animals could have come that way (1907:I, 46–47). Strachey, faced with the same problem three years later, gave the same answer: he referred his readers to Father Acosta (1953:55).

In such fashion the Acostan Tradition entered Northern scholarship on the subject of the origins of the Indians. In 1614 Edward Brerewood gave the tradition its earliest extended expression in English, if one discounts Edward Grimston's 1604 translation of *The Natural and Moral Historie of the Indies.* Brerewood's *Enquiries Touching the Diversity of Languages and Religions Through the Chief Parts of the World* was published at London in 1614. Purchas printed it in toto in his *Pilgrimes* twelve years later; new English editions also came out in 1622, 1635, and 1674. French editions appeared in 1640 and 1663, and Latin editions in 1650 and 1659. Brerewood was professor of astronomy at Gresham College, but his hobby was language analysis: his *Enquiries* was something of a landmark in the development of linguistics. He may have reached his conclusions independently as a result of his analyses, but he did know of Acosta's work and cited it near the beginning of his section on Indians (1614:98 n.).

Brerewood began his discussion of American natives with a long section on the Tatars. The Tatars, like many of the primitive peoples of the Earth, were frequently identified as the remnants of the Ten Lost Tribes of Israel. The evidence used to substantiate this claim resembled that used to prove the Indians descended from the Tribes: The word "Tatary" was actually "Totari," meaning "remnant" in Hebrew;

Tatars practiced circumcision, etc. Brerewood (1614:95–96) denied each of these evidences and the conclusions based on them; then he turned to America.

> And what if the innumerable people of so many nations, as are known to inhabit and overspread the huge continent of America, be also of the same of-spring [as the Tatars]? Certainly, if I be not greatly deceived, they are no other. For first, that their originall must be derived from Asia is apparent, because . . . they have no rellish nor resemblance at all, of the Arts, or learning, or civilitie of Europe: And their colour testifieth, they are not of the Africans progenie . . . (1614:96).

This lack of "arts or industrie" resembling those of the known civilized areas of Europe and Asia, the Indians' "grosse ignorance of letters," their idolatry, "incivilitie, and many barbarous properties" led Brerewood to conclude that the Americans descended from the Tatars (1614:96–97).

Brerewood did not argue solely on these grounds. The best argument of all, he thought, was geographical. The west coast of America, which lay nearest to Asia and the homeland of the Tatars, was also the most heavily populated side. Furthermore, "it is certain that the North-East part of Asia possessed by the Tatars, is if not continent with the west side of America . . . is the least disjoyned by Sea." By such a route came the "ravenous and harmlesse beasts . . . which men as is likely, would never to their owne harm transport" (1614:96–97).

Then Brerewood returned to the lost tribes theory of Indian-Tatar origins. He attempted to prove historically that such was impossible. Circumcision among the Tatars, he argued, was no older than their Mohammedanism; nor was circumcision peculiar to the Jews. Furthermore, he continued, Esdras was not authoritative: the Ten Tribes never left Assyria, and Arsareth was a myth (1614:98–108).

Samuel Purchas accepted Brerewood's arguments, and included the entire *Enquiries* in his *Haklaytus Posthumus, or Purchas His Pilgrimes* (London, 1625). Purchas also included most of the Grimston translation of Acosta's *Historia natural y moral*. Purchas had written concerning the origins of the American Indians as early as 1613 when he published his *Purchas his Pilgrimage, or Relations of the World and the*

Religions observed in all ages and places discovered, from the Creation unto this Present. Neither the first edition (1613:609–612) nor the expanded third edition (1617:902–905) contained much information on this point although Purchas did reject the Carthaginians and Welsh as progenitors of the Indians. The third edition (1617:904) carried a brief summary of Brerewood's argument for a Tatar origin, but Purchas did not at that time accept it. By 1625, when *Purchas His Pilgrimes* appeared, Purchas had largely accepted Brerewood's thesis.

Purchas grounded his own version of the plantation of men in America in the works of Acosta, and of Brerewood. He evidently considered Brerewood's Tatar thesis a logical expansion of Acosta's arguments, and (1905–1906:I, 61–80) did not differ with Brerewood on the source of the Indians' ancestors. His attention focused on a rejection of older theories and an elaboration of the period in history when the first settlers went to the Indies. The sparse population of America indicated to Purchas that men went to the New World comparatively late in history. Unless men grew from stones or rained from clouds, Purchas (1905–1906:81–82) could not understand "how wise and learned men . . . fill China and America with people in those days before Moses and Abraham, and find great commerce and knowledge of the New World, when the Old was but yesterday begun." He repeated these arguments much later, adding that America was lately peopled, and that the population came by stages (1905–1906:I, 159–165).

If the Americans did indeed descend from the barbarous Tatars, how did they acquire such civilizations as Mexico and Peru? Purchas advanced a rather curious theory about the effects of climate on man and his culture-building. Northern climes made people "unquiet" of mind, bold, and forward; the "neere propinquity to the Sunne, Climates more temperate, richer Soyle, consent of elements and Aliments bred content to their minds and more prosperous concent of Fortunes, which softened their rigid dispositions, and by degrees disposed them to thinke on mechanicall and politike Arts, further to humanize their society, and to polish their cohabitation with politie" (1905–1906:I, 162).

Lescarbot, Strachey, Brerewood, and Purchas relied heavily on Acosta. The first did so to explain the knotty problem of animals in

America; the others used Acosta's geographical and faunal consideration to support their own theories. The Frenchman, despite Acosta,
accepted a trans-Atlantic "probability," while the English writers rejected it in favor of the Anian route. Not all English writers held to
that route: Thomas Morton, champion of the Trojan Indians, thought
such a route improbable because of the "frozen sea" (1947:16).

In 1589 Acosta had hinted that the Indian civilizations might be
native to America—that they might have developed after the original
settlers arrived. Brerewood did not consider this point, but a certain
degree of cultural autocthony seems implicit in his derivation of the
Indians from the barbarous Tatars. Purchas explicitly endorsed the
independent development of the higher civilizations of America; but
even he did not consider the question of autocthony as such.

The line of reasoning which led Brerewood and Purchas to choose
Tatary as the source of the American population amply illustrates the
strength of the type of argument this writer has labeled "Acostan." (In
this case the label is clearly warranted by their acknowledgements of
Acosta). Despite Brerewood's endorsement of certain similarities between Indians and Tatars, he considered that his secondary argument.
His reasoning took the form of eliminating possibilities. Geography
and skin color eliminated Africa. Geography and extreme differences
in cultural levels eliminated Europe. Geography and related faunal
considerations pointed to Asia as the likely source. The fact that the
Tatars possessed the land nearest to America, and the fact that they resembled each other in general cultural level, suggested that the Indians
were merely Tatars who had moved to America. Brerewood did not
allow his great interest in languages to lead him into a comparison of
Indian and Tatar languages.

Perhaps the lack of a vast trans-Atlantic migration of the English,
such as Spain had experienced in the sixteenth century, made it easier
for Brerewood, Purchas, and Strachey to reject such migrations in pre-
Columbian times. Even the Madoc legend mentioned by Hakluyt, Purchas (1613:610), and later by John Smith (1808–1814:XIII, 2)
found no support.

The Acostan Tradition appeared stronger in England before the
Lost Tribes furor of the 1640's and 1650's than in Spain itself. The

Brerewood statement of 1614 appeared about the same time as Herrera
(1601–1613) and Torquemada (1613) in Spain. But the Brerewood
position was essentially stronger because it was unencumbered by the
morass of the Garcían or trans-Atlantic traditions. Lescarbot had introduced Acosta to the French in 1609, but the French showed a strange
lack of interest in the origins of the Indians. So far as this writer could
ascertain, the first book in French on the subject was E. Bailli d'Engel's
*Essai sur cette question: Quand et comment l'Amerique a-t-elle été
peuplée d'hommes et d'animaux* (Amsterdam, 1767).

The Grotius-De Laet Controversy

The question of the origin of the natives of the New World seldom
produced arguments of the polemical type. The entire Spanish literature on the subject reveals no such arguments. A theory might have to
wait several years for a refutation, while the counter-refutation, usually
not by the original author, would follow some years later, if at all. If
confrontations either personal or literary did occur, they were unknown
and unpublished. Fernando Colón's attack on Oviedo might have resulted in a polemic, but Fernando's book was not published while the
two men still lived.

The first literary confrontation on the subject of Indian origins began in 1641. Because it involved Hugo Grotius, the "father of inter-
national law," it has become by far the best known incident in the early
history of the search for Indian origins (Meulin, 1950:326–327;
Wright, 1928; Imbelloni, 1956:55; Winsor, 1889:369–370). The
major figures in the controversy other than Grotius were a fellow-
Dutchman, Joannes de Laet, and a German-turned-Dutchman, Georg
Horn. Neither De Laet nor Horn enjoyed as much fame as Grotius, but
they were important men in their own right.

Jan, or Joannes, de Laet was a man of considerable stature in Holland when the controversy began. For many years he had served as a
director of the Dutch West India Company and naturally, as a consequence of that association, had a strong interest in any subject touching
on America. He also reportedly had a daughter who had emigrated to
New Amsterdam. But De Laet's reputation rested not so much on his

commercial connections as upon his literary activity (Wright, 1928: 214–218; Eyries, 1854–1865b:439–440).

By 1640 De Laet had already written a history of the Dutch West India Company and some popular geographical-travel books on Spain, France, Portugal, Persia, Turkey, England, and Eastern Europe. He had published too a valuable history of the New World that appeared in Dutch (1625 and 1630) and Latin (1633), and in a French translation in 1640. De Laet's work with the West India Company, his association with the important publishing house of the Elzeviers in Leyden, and his wide interests brought him into contact with many of the more influential men in Holland (Wright, 1928:214–218).

Georg Horn was a much younger man than either Grotius or De Laet. He was only in his early twenties in 1641 (Grotius was 59, De Laet 58), and he took no public part in the debate as it happened. But he did write a book on the subject at the instigation of De Laet. The death of Grotius in 1644 and other circumstances prevented the publication of Horn's volume until 1652. One of those circumstances was his work as a professor of history at Leyden, where he was employed after 1648 (Wright, 1928:227–228; Eyries, 1854–1865a:640–641).

Horn's reputation now is based mainly on his polemics; the most famous of which was his pamphlet war with Isaac Vos in 1659. The subject was the "True Age of the Earth." Vos argued for 2256 years before the Flood; Horn allowed only 1440. In all, Vos produced four pamphlets of "castigationes," and "defensiones"; Horn wrote three (Eyries, 1854–1865a:640–641).

Late in 1641 Hugo Grotius, then serving as Swedish ambassador to Paris, completed a small pamphlet, *De Origine Gentium Americanarum*. Grotius sent the manuscript to his brother with the request that he show it to his fellow-countryman, Joannes de Laet, whom he knew to be an expert on America. Moreover, Grotius asked his brother not to reveal the identity of the author. The brother gave the manuscript to a relative of De Laet, who in turn took it to De Laet himself. De Laet read the pamphlet, wrote some notes on various points, and returned it to its author by the same route he had received it. With it he sent his notes, a Mexican vocabulary, and a copy of Acosta's *Historia* in Spanish (Wright, 1928:224; Meulin, 1950:326). Grotius published his pamphlet in the spring of 1642 without altering the original text. At least two, and possibly four, editions of the *Origine* appeared before the end of the year. None showed any consideration of the material De Laet had sent to Grotius.

De Origine Gentium Americanarum contained fifteen small pages. Grotius began by erroneously stating that "no one from among so many learned men of our age has earnestly investigated whence those nations sprung which" inhabited America. Since he had read several of the Spanish, French, English, and Dutch writers who had been to America, he proposed to offer a solution. He invited other scholars who "may possess a greater knowledge of these events" to confirm or refute his arguments (1884:8).

Grotius (1884:10–14) proposed that the Indians north of the Isthmus of Panama (except for Yucatán) descended from Norwegians. He based this conclusion largely on word comparisons. Iceland, Greenland, Frisland, Estotiland all ended with the German (Norse) suffix signifying "land." Then he pointed out various place-names in Mexico which possessed the same ending: Cimatlan, Cuatlan, Tenuchitlan, Ocotlan, et al. In like manner he presented words such as "Teut" (God), "waiert" (lash) and "beke" (stream) which were common to the Germans (which included the Dutch) and the Indians of North America. He concluded his evidence for a Norse (German) origin with a catalogue of cultural similarities totally lacking in novelty.

Yucatán was a special case. The practice of circumcision there proved to Grotius that the natives must have descended from some Old World people who used that practice. He rejected the Lost Tribes theory because Esdras was "full of vain dreams" (1884:14). He finally settled on Ethiopia as the source of the Yucatecan people because the Ethiopians, though a Christian people, had retained circumcision. This theory would account for that practice and also for the presence of "crosses" on Cozumel (1884:15–17).

Grotius thought "the more highly refined minds of the Peruvians" as well as their other finer qualities indicated that they descended from the Chinese. His major argument in support of this contention was that both Chinese and Peruvians wrote in characters and from the top down. Language differences resulted from mixtures and deterioration (1884:17–20).

In the process of creating his own theories, Grotius rejected all others—especially those calling for a land route:

It is certain that before the arrival of the Spaniards there were no horses in all America. Now Scythia is a country always full of horses, and almost all Scythians are accustomed to ride horseback. . . . And if America and Tartary were united together, the horses . . . would long ago have forced their way from Tartary to America. . . . But if a continual strait intervened, as I rather believe, Tartary never had navigators, and if she had them, never would they have crossed without horses, or been content to remain long without them (1884:9–10).

All Grotius' settlers were rather late arrivals in America. He did not even consider the possibility that the Indians might have gone to the New World before the time of Christ, before the Norse got to Greenland, or before the Scythians-Tatars domesticated the horse. Indeed, his concept of Scythia was somewhat outdated. Europeans had long since telescoped Scythia (originally north and east of the Black Sea) and Tatary into one place. Scythia-Tatary presumably stretched from the vicinity of the Black Sea to the Straits of Anian (Bering), and most Europeans assumed that whatever held true for near-Tatary also held true for far-Tatary.

The rejection of geographical considerations and the evidence of the animals were two of the points De Laet suggested Grotius reconsider. For that reason De Laet sent him a copy of Acosta's *Historia natural y moral*. Grotius' failure to use any of De Laet's notes and his failure to consider Acosta's arguments irritated De Laet. He was also angered by the insult implicit in the fact that Grotius had solicited his advice and not made use of it (Wright, 1928:224).

Joannes de Laet had long since accepted the arguments of Joseph de Acosta. In the "Preface" to the French edition of his history of the New World (Paris, 1640), he stated that "we will not speak of how or whence the savages and inhabitants are firstly come in those regions." He referred the interested reader to Acosta's *Historia natural y moral*.

De Laet elaborated his opinion much more fully in his *Notae ad Dissertationem Hugonis Grotii* published at Amsterdam in 1643. His approach involved printing Grotius' pamphlet in annotated form, considering and rejecting, or at least questioning, each idea or statement in turn. De Laet saw no reason to differentiate between Indians north and south of the Isthmus of Panama, pointing out that the Spanish, who knew most about the Indians, did not make such a distinction (Ogilby, 1671:30). Furthermore, he said, the Mexicans and Teutons did not use the endings "land" and "lan" in the same sense. Some of the other words Grotius compared were incorrect. "Waiert" meant "fan," not "lash"; and its American equivalent ("Guaira") was used only in Grotius' Chinese Peru (Ogilby, 1671:30–32). Grotius thought the Mexicans used the Dutch word "beke" (rivulet) in the form "peke." De Laet pointed out that the Mexican word for rivulet was actually *atlauhtli*. The annotator then inserted a long vocabulary showing a lack of correspondence between several European languages and such American languages as those of the Mexicans (Nahuatl) and Iroquois (Ogilby, 1671:33; Wright, 1928:222).

De Laet then turned his attention to the Chinese in Peru. Nowhere in Peru, he maintained, could one find artisans such as those in China so esteemed by the world. And why should the Chinese go only to Peru when China was much closer to New Spain? De Laet also knew something about Confucianism, and argued that the Chinese religion did not resemble the Peruvian. Finally, argued De Laet, are we to compare the Chinese language with its several types of characters, its eighty-thousand monosyllabic words, and its dictionaries, to the language of a people who "know neither Pen, Paper, Ink" and who "reckon the antiquity of time by strung beads?" (Ogilby, 1671:34–35).

De Laet used his *Notae* to express his own opinion and to show the fallacy of Grotius' thinking with regard to various origin theories, especially the Tatar-Scythian thesis. Grotius misstated the argument, he maintained,

For two questions must be considered here: 'Who could have come to the New World?' and 'How could they have come?' Both questions must have a satisfactory answer, if the puzzle is to be solved correctly. Those who hold that the Indians came from Scythia or Great Tartary do not necessarily mean that they were Scythians or of Scythian origin, for they may mean peoples dispossessed and driven out by the Scythians. . . . Consequently, the arguments which Grotius bases upon this hypothesis, arguments which are drawn from the genius and customs of the Scythian people, do not refute the opinion intended.

But, granting Grotius' supposition for the sake of argument, he went too far in basing his claim against the Scythian origin on the statement that there were no horses in America before the arrival of the Spaniards. . . . The fact that Scythia was then full of horses does not prove that such was always the case or that such was the case when the supposed transmigration occurred, which must have happened many centuries ago, because the vast multitudes of men in America differ so much in their geniuses, languages, customs, morals, and the propagation of such vast numbers must have taken many centuries. Consequently, the inference is easy that the transmigration took place long ago, and immediately after the dispersion in Asia, on account of the confusion of tongues (quoted in Wright, 1928:220–222).

Only the assumption of an ancient origin for the Indians could explain all the differences in languages.

Although De Laet thought the earliest settlers came from Scythia-Tatary, he did not rule out the possibility of later arrivals (Engel, 1767:I, 7–11; Wright, 1928:221–222), but the late-comers were probably not Christian. Among the possibilities he admitted were the Madoc story, perhaps some Polynesians, and maybe some tempest-driven Spaniards from the Canaries. All these were minor additions (Wright, 1928:222).

Grotius took De Laet's criticism rather badly, and replied "avec beaucoup de hauteur," in a thirty-five page pamphlet called *De Origine Gentium Americanarum Dissertatio Altera* (Paris and Amsterdam, 1643). Some of the copies of this pamphlet evidently included an unidentified portrait of De Laet labeled "Adversus obtrectatorem opaca bonum quem facit barba," from Catullus' "against an envious detractor, whom a shadowy beard makes good"—an allusion to De Laet's Capuchin-like beard (Meulen, 1950:329; Wright, 1928:222–223).

Grotius made no serious attempt to reply to De Laet's *Notae* in his second dissertation. He said of De Laet that "everything he has written against me, he has written with a desire not for truth, but for detraction." He spent his pamphlet reviling his annotator and accusing him of being a controversialist (Wright, 1928:222–223).

De Laet answered the *Dissertatio Altera* in the same fashion as he had answered the first, in his *Responsio ad Dissertationem Secundum Hugonis Grotii* (Amsterdam, 1644). In this *Responsio*, De Laet revealed his reason for publishing his original *Notae:* i.e., the solicited but unused advice. He said also that despite what Grotius did in the future, he would make no additional reply. De Laet repeated much of the argument from the *Notae*, but with considerably more evidence to disprove both the probability of an Ethiopian origin and other points made by Grotius (Wright, 1928:226).

Neither Grotius nor De Laet personally continued their controversy. Meulen (1950:330) indicated, however, that Grotius (who died later in 1644) decided to persuade others to respond for him. And Horn in the "Preface" to his *De Originibus Americanis*, published in 1652, claimed the book was written originally at De Laet's instigation several years before the latter's death in 1649 (Meulen, 1950:330; Wright, 1928:227–228). Grotius' champion is unknown and may not have completed his work. Several other writers, however, did produce books directed toward the Grotius-De Laet controversy. One of them was Jean Baptiste Poissons, whose *Animadversiones ad ea quae Hugo Grotius et Johannes Lahetius de Origine Gentium Peruvianarum et Mexicanarum scripserunt* appeared at Paris in 1644. In this brief pamphlet of perhaps two-thousand words, Poissons (1644:6–7) cites the cosmographer Genebrard and the biblical scholars Arias Montano and Postel in support of the Ophirian theory.

Also in 1644, the pamphlet *De Origine Americanarum Dissertatio* by Robert Comte (Roberti Comtaeus) appeared posthumously at Amsterdam. John Ogilby (1671:18–27) made several lengthy references to Comte's arguments: "With many Learned and seemingly true Arguments [he] affirms, that the Original of the *Americans* must be sought for either among the Phoenicians, Sydonians, Tyrians, or Carthaginians, being all are one people" (1671:18). Comte's method consisted of referring to all ancient statements concerning what might be the

Indies, and comparing common elements in the Carthaginian-Indian religion, economy, customs, polity, and language. Georg Horn claimed that Comte intended to write an extended work weighing the arguments of De Laet and Grotius, but that he died before he could do so (Wright, 1928:227, n. 52). Whether it was to be a separate work or a continuation of the first was not clear.

Georg Horn published his own book in 1652. His position was essentially the same as De Laet's. Engel, who in 1767 began his discussion of earlier theories with Grotius, found De Laet's and Horn's theories so similar that he discussed them as a unit (1767:I, 5–11). Barcia (García, 1729: "Proemio") charged that Horn wrote and published his book so hurriedly that he failed to produce a "mature" book, or to specify his sources: "an ancient vice of the Heretics." This accusation seems largely true, despite what Horn said in his "Preface" and the fact that Barcia used the second printing of 1669, and did not know of the 1652 edition.

The literary consequences of this dispute did not end with Horn. The subject of the origins of the American Indians became a very important one after mid-century. In part this was due to the notoriety of the Grotius-De Laet dispute; in part to the intrinsic interest of the subject. This writer has gathered references to numerous books touching on the subject, some of which are not verifiable. George Kaspar Kirchmaier upheld the Anian route with some Phoenician additions in a *Disputatio geográphico-histórico de Origine aditu atque fama gentium Americanarum* in 1659 (Allen, 1949:129–130). Godofredus Wagner argued a similar position in his doctoral examination of 1669 at Leipzig. The New York Public Library credits this book, *De Originibus Americanis,* to Johann H. Horb, the chairman of Wagner's committee. Another pro-Anian *Dissertatio de origine gentium novi orbis prima* by Ericus Ljung of Upsala, Sweden (1676), is likewise credited to the chairman, Claudius Arrhenius Ornhielm (Allen, 1949:130, n. 84).

The Grotius-De Laet controversy and the works related to it illustrate the strength of the Acostan Tradition in northern Europe at mid-century. Joannes de Laet and Georg Horn, as well as some other authors, followed the arguments based on geography and animal distribution first laid down by Acosta in 1589. They went further than the Spaniard and identified the area of origination more precisely as Siberia (Tatary-Scythia), even though the first Indians might have been non-Tatars pushed out of Tatary and into America by the Tatars.

The northern elaboration of the Acostan argument produced a position which may be stated thusly: because of the geographical isolation of America from Europe and Africa, the first settlers must have come from Asia. The presence in the New World of animals which could not have come in ships with men from Europe also indicated an Asian origin, while the presence of the same animals argued that America was either connected to Asia by land, or only narrowly separated by water. The size of the total population of America, and the variety of languages indicated a great antiquity for the original settlement. Consequently, it could be assumed that the Indians who originally came to America from Tatary might not be related to the tribes historically known to inhabit that region. Or, if the Indians were descendants of the historic Tatars, their antiquity indicated that they probably came before the Tatars developed some of their current cultural baggage, such as the domesticated horse. The Indians might then be derived from some unknown tribe which once lived in Tatary.

If such reasoning is true, it would of course be impossible to discover which *people* gave rise to the American Indians. The best one could do would be to assume that the unknown tribe (or tribes) from which the Indians descended more or less resembled the tribes which currently lived in Tatary.

This argument had the same effect as Acosta's hint of cultural autocthony: that is, it would make ultimate derivation of the Indians impossible except on a strictly geographical basis. And the autocthony was still there, for the unknown tribe probably did not possess a high civilization. The factors behind the source of the high cultures of Mexico and Peru remained unresolved. Did the savages produce such cultures independently?

Purchas (1905–1906:I, 162) had endorsed climate as the determining factor in the production of Indian civilizations. But the Genesis-based traditions of diffusionism were too strong for most men. Both

De Laet and Horn were ready to grant a large measure of autocthony; but, as Barcia pointed out (García, 1729:242), Horn was uncertain that the Indians could have invented architecture and other arts.

By 1650 the writers in the Acostan Tradition were willing to derive the Indians from some unknown tribe in northeastern Asia, at an unknown, but ancient, time. This position is substantially identical to that accepted by most modern authorities. But the Acostans were not able to maintain this position. Scholarly opinion of the day did not admit the possibility of genuinely unknown tribes. Since all tribes were related through common descent from Adam by way of Noah and his sons and all tribes could be traced to their relations, the possibility of a "wild state" for men was not in conformity with theology.

The Acostans could argue that tribes might be unknown in the sense that their relationship to other tribes might not be traceable, but culture was another matter. Regardless of how strongly their reasoning suggested autocthony, the knowledge and beliefs of the time could scarcely support an extreme statement of that position (Hodgen, 1964). So Horn and De Laet, as had Brerewood, Acosta himself, and Acosta's Spanish followers, admitted the possibility of late-comers of the "trans-Atlantic" sort.

One can glimpse the beginning of a certain clarification about the origin of the natives of the New World in the first half of the seventeenth century. At mid-century the question where the Indians had come from appeared to be in the process of separating from the question of their cultural origins. Not that there was any clear recognition of this possibility at the time, for these two aspects of the origin problem did not fully separate until the nineteenth century, and the cultural-origins concept has largely dominated the literature in this century.

Though the possibility of separate physical and cultural origins of the Indians was emerging in the seventeenth century, it had little influence on the literature. The old habit of mind which ascribed men and culture to the same origin continued to dominate the discussion. Even the Acostans who had to resort to late-arriving Mediterraneans to explain the high cultures of America do not appear to have recognized the implications of this necessity to the idea of a single physical and cultural origin. Nor did they seem to realize that such a resort, without the separation of physical and cultural origins, could lead them straight to the all-embracing Garcían position.

The Jews in America and the Hope of Israel, 1644–1660

The Grotius-De Laet affair was not the only controversy of importance involving the origins of the American Indians. Indeed, that controversy was important only in itself: its repercussions were apparently entirely personal and theoretical. At the time this controversy raged in the mid-1640's, an argument of far greater practical application began to take shape in Holland and England. The points at issue, at first glance apparently unrelated, were, "Are the American Indians Hebrew?" and "Should the Jews be re-admitted to England?"

In late 1644 a Portuguese Jew Antonio Montesinos (Aahron Levi) arrived in Amsterdam with a truly marvelous tale. While in the province of Popayán in southern Nueva Granada in 1641, he had hired some mules and Indians to take him into the mountains of Quito province. Among the Indians was a "cacique" named Francisco. On the occasion of a storm, Francisco remarked to Montesinos that the Indians had once offended a "Holy People," and that storm, like the Spaniards, was part of their punishment (Manasseh, 1652:1).

Montesinos did not pursue the matter at that time. Later he was imprisoned by the Inquisition at Cartagena. During one of his prayers in prison, when he started to give thanks for not having become a barbarian or an Indian, he mistakenly said that Hebrews were Indians. By a very circuitous route, this brought him back to the cryptic comments of Francisco about the "Holy People." On his release he looked up Francisco and confessed to the Indian that he was a Hebrew. In time Francisco led him to the "Holy People," still hidden in the mountains (Manasseh, 1652:2–3).

These hidden people were Jews, brought to the area "by the providence of God." The Indians had made war on them initially, but they had failed, and eventually the natives became followers of the Jews. Then the Spanish came, so the Indians kept their Judaism secret. These hidden Jews revealed to Antonio that they would soon emerge, cast out the Spanish, and reunite with Israel (Manasseh, 1652:3–7).

Montesinos' story caused a great stir among the Jews of Amsterdam. Some questioned the traveler's veracity; as a result he was examined by the leaders of the Amsterdam Jews and certified to be of good character. The story spread beyond the Jewish community and attracted the attention of many gentiles, some of whom began to write to Amsterdam to find out the details of Montesinos' story. The man to whom they most frequently wrote was the Rabbi Manasseh ben Israel.

Manasseh ben Israel was, like Montesinos, a Portuguese Jew. He was born on the island of Madeira about 1604, but had moved to Amsterdam as a boy. He became a theology student and a rabbi at the age of eighteen. But Manasseh was not content with a routine life. He studied languages avidly. In addition to his native Portuguese and Spanish, which was the language of the Amsterdam Jews, Manasseh learned Hebrew, Latin, English, French, Dutch, and at least three other languages. He also established a Hebrew press in Amsterdam and was for a generation the leading printer of Hebrew language material in Europe (Roth, 1945). But his prime interests were literary. In 1632 he published at Frankfort the first volume of his *Conciliador*, in Spanish. This volume on the consistency of the Scriptures brought Manasseh to the attention of gentile scholars and made him somewhat fashionable (Roth, 1945:44).

Jewish scholars were generally not highly regarded in gentile Europe, but Manasseh was accepted. He became a close friend of Isaac Vos (who later conducted the polemic *De Vera Aetate Mundi* with Georg Horn) and he occasionally corresponded with Hugo Grotius (Roth, 1945:59, 143–148). He may have known De Laet and Horn, since he engaged in the West Indian trade as did De Laet and possessed interests similar to theirs. On two occasions Manasseh was painted by Rembrandt.

Manasseh wrote several other books in Spanish and Latin which increased his fame, and he was also one of the Jewish leaders who examined Montesinos' character. Consequently, it was natural that gentiles interested in the story should write to Manasseh for information. When he began to receive requests for the Montesinos story he apparently wrote out a *Relación* of the tale to send to his correspondents. One of the men who requested the Montesinos *Relación* was John

Dury, an English theologian of some note who had met Manasseh when Dury was in Holland as Chaplain to Mary Stuart, Princess of Orange (Dury, 1650; Roth, 1945:181).

Dury's interest in the Jewish-Indian theory derived from a friendship with Thomas Thorowgood, rector of Grimston in Norfolk. In 1648 Thorowgood composed a little book called *Iewes in America* and sent the manuscript to Dury for his criticism. Dury replied in a long *Epistolicall Discourse* urging Thorowgood to publish his book. He also passed along what information he possessed on the subject and detailed his efforts to get more (Dury, 1650).

One of those efforts involved contacting Manasseh ben Israel about the rumors he had heard concerning the *Relación* of Montesinos. Manasseh sent him a copy; the *Relación* raised several additional questions, prompting Dury to write to Manasseh asking him to elaborate on certain points. Manasseh's reply took the form of a book which he advised Dury he intended to publish (Dury, 1650; Roth, 1945:183–184; Hyamson, 1903:660–662).

Manasseh's venture into the Jewish-Indian theory was far more complex than most such endeavors. One of the most delicate aspects of Manasseh's contact with gentiles was their frequent insistence on attempting his conversion. Sometimes these attempts were based on the belief that the millenium was near and Israel must be converted before it could be ushered in. At the time Manasseh became interested in writing a book about the American Indians he was in contact with gentiles of such messianic persuasions (Roth, 1945:184–185).

Manasseh began to make a connection between the supposed discovery of the Lost Tribes of Israel in America and his own messianic traditions. Did not the Scriptures indicate that the Messiah could not come until the dispersion of Israel was completed? Thus, when Manasseh's book appeared in 1650 it bore the Latin title *Spes Israelis— The Hope of Israel* (Roth, 1945:185).

Judged only by the number of editions, the volume by Manasseh was by far the most popular in the literature on Indian origins. The Latin edition appeared in early 1650. By the end of the year two Spanish-language editions (rewritten in Spanish by Manasseh as *Esto es Esperanza de Israel*) and an English translation by Moses Wall (as *The*

Hope of Israel) had also appeared. The Spanish version was reprinted in 1659, 1723, 1881, and 1929. The English edition reappeared in 1651, 1652, 1792, 1850, and 1901. In addition there were two Dutch editions in 1666; Judeo-German versions in 1691 and two editions in 1712; and at least eight Hebrew versions, two of which appeared before 1703 (Roth, 1945:301–302).

Manasseh was the first Jew to write a study concerning the origins of the American Indians, and apparently one of the first Jews to accept the Jewish-origin theory (Hyamson, 1903:656). His arguments were largely a rehash of the older writings on the Lost Tribes theory. He admitted, as had previous commentators, that the problem of discovering origins posed many difficulties. Then he systematically rejected other theories—Carthage, Ophir, et al.—and concluded that those Spaniards who inhabited the Indies generally regarded the Indians as descendants of Jews, and that they were correct (1881:18–23).

According to Manasseh's version of the Lost Tribes theory, the Israelites got to the New World first, but late-coming gentiles drove them into the mountains. The Jewish characteristics evident among the later arrivals resulted from their contact with the Jews (1881:23–24). Next he proceeded with the Esdras story and the supporting similarities between the Indians and the Jews (1881:24–83). He concluded with the reasons which compelled him to believe the discovery of the Lost Tribes in America signalized that the day of redemption for Israel was near (1881:83–114).

Manasseh concluded: (1) that the Indies were anciently inhabited by part of the Ten Tribes who came via the Straits of Anian and some of whom still lived hidden in unknown parts of America; (2) that not all the Ten Tribes came to the New World, but that some dispersed to other parts of the world; (3) that they did not return to the second Temple; (4) that to this day the Lost Tribes kept the Jewish religion; (5) that the prophecies of their return to their own land would be fulfilled; (6) that they would return to Jerusalem; and (7) that the Twelve Tribes would be united (1881:114–115).

At about the same time Manasseh published his *Spes Israelis* in Amsterdam, Thomas Thorowgood finally published in London his *Iewes in America, or, Probabilities that the Americans are of that Race*.

Thorowgood's volume lay more nearly in the tradition of the dispute over Jewish Indians. He used much of his space to describe why he thought the Indians were Jews. He based his opinion on seven considerations: (1) native myths, which he thought indicated a Jewish origin; (2) similar common, or profane, customs; (3) similar sacred rites; (4) speech; (5) the presence of cannibalism prophesied in the Bible; (6) Indians were the last to know Christ, as the Jews were supposed to be the last; and (7) the calamities and hardships of the Indians which the Bible prophesied for the Jews (1650:6–35).

The millenialist element was also very pronounced in Thorowgood's writing:

> From the Jews our faith began,
> To the Gentiles then it ran,
> To the Jews return it shall,
> Before the dreadful end of all.
>   (1650:24)

After a brief "Part II," devoted to answering a few standard objections, Thorowgood wrote a long essay called "Earnest desires for effectual endeavours to make them Christians." Montesinos' *Relación* appeared at the end of the volume in an English translation.

The desire of the millenialists to Christianize the Jews in order to hasten "the dreadful end of all," and Thorowgood's missionary zeal to convert the Indians by supporting the work of John Eliot, the "Apostle to the Indians," served to draw considerable attention to the Jewish question and to subordinate the Indian origin question to it. There was in England a strong and growing opinion that the best way to convert the Jews was to allow them to reenter England whence they had been legally barred since 1290 (Roth, 1945:188–202; Hyamson, 1903:667–676).

This idea meshed well with Manasseh's own thinking. The "Hope of Israel"—the Messiah—could not come until the Jews were dispersed to the ends of the Earth. Since they had been found in America, and since the oppressions accompanying the "Coming" were apparent, it became more and more vital to return the Jews to England. In medieval Jewish tradition the word "England" meant "the end of the Earth";

therefore, it was especially necessary to return there to complete the dispersion. Manasseh may have begun his investigations of the Jewish Indians out of curiosity, but they had led him to a mystical position wherein the Indians became secondary to "the Hope of Israel" (Roth, 1945:201–208).

The Hope of Israel proved useful to Manasseh's plans for securing the return of the Jews to England. The three English editions of 1650, 1651, and 1652 all carried his dedication "To the Parliament, the Supreme Court of England, and to the Right Honourable the Council of State," which hinted at the possibility of Jewish readmission. The last two editions contained some "Considerations upon the point of the Conversion of the Jews," consisting of correspondence on that subject between the translator, Moses Wall, and one Edward Spenser.

The subsequent development of the readmission controversy, Manasseh's journey to England in an unsuccessful attempt to persuade Cromwell to negotiate reentry, and the eventual readmission under Charles II, all well chronicled by Cecil Roth (1945) and Wolf (1901), lie beyond the scope of this essay.

Thomas Thorowgood's *Iewes in America* was not completely lost in the readmission crisis, though it did take second place to Manasseh's *Hope of Israel*. His fellow-theologian, Hamon l'Estrange, took sufficient notice of it to denounce it (along with Manasseh's book) in his *Americans no Iewes, or, Improbabilities that the Americans are of that Race*, probably published at London in 1651, though the date reads 1652. L'Estrange thought that the Indians, whom he argued were descendants of Shem (1652:8–9), went to America long before the Ten Tribes became lost. His refutation of Thorowgood took the form of denying each of the supposed similarities point by point and showing that the characteristics compared were not peculiar to the Jews or to Indians (1652:13–80).

L'Estrange drew freely from Brerewood in his argument against the Jewish Indians. Indeed, he said, if he decided to change his opinion, Brerewood's Tatarian origin seemed the next most reasonable. Despite this criticism, Thorowgood's book was apparently reprinted in 1652 (Sabin, 95650). Thorowgood, however, did not publish anything new on the subject until 1660. In that year he published his *Jews in Ameri-*

ca, or, Probabilities that those Indians are Judaical . . . at London. It
was reprinted later the same year (Sabin, 95653).

Thorowgood took the time in this second book to elaborate on what
he meant by the word "probability." Though "Aristotle defines that
to be probable which seems to be true," Thorowgood offered a somewhat different definition.

A Theme, Sentence, or Problem is said to be probable, when it cannot certainly be affirmed or denied, but the assent of the Reader, or Hearer is left
to the weight of those arguments or examples which are laid before him,
and are most prevalent with his reason (1660:10–11).

Apparently he meant something akin to the modern concept of possible.

Jews in America contained sixty-seven pages of new testimony on
such things as circumcision, language, and customs. He added nothing
new in itself in this book, but only items which he had overlooked the
first time. He did, however, include "The Learned Conjecture of
Reverend John Eliot Touching the Americans" which endorsed the
Lost Tribes theory. As with his earlier *Iewes in America,* Thorowgood
devoted much space to missionary considerations.

The literary discussion of the Lost Tribes of Israel and the American
Indians between 1650 and 1660 was oriented largely toward theology
and evangelism, rather than toward a consideration of the origins of
the Indians as an intellectual problem, nor did the controversy serve to
invigorate the Lost Tribes theory. The American Samuel Sewall wrote
in 1686 that Thorowgood's "arguments are not easily avoided," and
again in 1696 that "Mr. Eliot and Mr. Thorowgood with many others
are of the opinion that the Ten Tribes are here, and their arguments
are not frivolous" (Sewall, 1886–1888:22–23, 177). Cotton Mather
also knew of Thorowgood's work, but he jokingly spoke of men who
looked for Jews among the Indians for "thorow-good" reasons (1820:
I, 506).

The discussion of the Lost Tribes theory in Europe was much more
vigorous; but it was also more generally negative. Charles Rochefort's
History of the Caribby Islands (Paris, 1658; London, 1666) referred
to the Jewish-Indian argument as grounding "an imagination on too

weak conjectures" (1666:206–207). John Ogilby (1671:27–29) rejected the theory in his *America*. Gottlieb Spitzel (Spizelius) wrote so thorough a denunciation of the Lost Tribes origin theory in his *Elevatio relationis Montezinianae* ... of 1661, that Allen (1949:128) thought he "was successful in burying the theory of the Indians as descendants of the Ten Lost Tribes as deep as the great abyss."

The conclusion seems inescapable that the flurry of books on the Lost Tribes theory of Indian origins between 1650 and 1661 did little to advance the general discussion of Indian origins. The political and messianic overtones of the affair detracted from its potential ethnographic impact. Many people in Europe and America no doubt agreed with Manasseh and Thorowgood, and many were probably convinced by their books. But the writers who continued the discussion of Indian origins in later years showed no great desire to adopt the Jewish-Indian argument.

John Ogilby wrote the first substantial investigation of the various origin theories after the "Hope of Israel" incident in his *America* (London, 1671). He began with a rejection of the possibility that the ancients knew of America; then he turned his attention to the "several Opinions, and the Learned still Jangling" (1671:5–12). Ogilby argued that the Indians must have come to America at a very ancient date. The presence of certain arts, such as goldsmithy, indicated the natives had been settled long enough to develop arts (1671:12). The Indians must also have traveled to the New World by land, for "what profit could tygers, Lions, Wolves, Bears, and the like advantage the Transporter?" (1671:13–16).

Ogilby knew that Greenland and "Friezland" lay near America "but not without vast Bays and Inlets, which betwixt *Groenland* and *America* are obstructed with floating Castles of Ice." The first migration, he argued, must have come from Tatary (1671:30, 37–39): "Tartary ... certainly was the first nursery from whence the *Americans* were Transplanted." The modern Tatars were descendants of the Jews, he thought. "Yet nevertheless, the *Israelites* are not to be taken for the Planters of America ... America was inhabited long before the dispersion of the Israelites" (1671:39).

But Ogilby did not leave the population of America to some un-known tribe. He thought the Scythians—the ancient inhabitants of Tatary—produced the Indians. He offered in evidence of this claim several characteristics common to both. In addition to the standard cultural comparisons, Ogilby argued that the very diversity of practices among the Indians and Scythians was indicative of a relationship. He noted the width between the eyes, the medium stature, and the downy hair of the chin, which he thought indicated a common ancestry (1671: 39–42). He did not use language comparisons: "It in no way follows that one people take original from the other, because here and there are several words found, that have the same signification and [are] found in divers countreys" (1671:32).

John Ogilby relied frequently on Horn, De Laet, and Purchas; and through the work of these men he knew Brerewood and Acosta. Ogilby, like the men mentioned above, rejected those who thought the first Indians came across the sea. But he admitted that America was peopled on a continual basis, and some late-comers might have gone there by sea (1671:36–37). In general, Ogilby's position closely paralleled that of De Laet.

John Josselyn, in *An Account of Two Voyages* published three years after Ogilby, adopted the Tatar origin theory. "The people that inhabit this countrey are judged to be of the *Tartars* called *Samonids* that border upon *Muscovia* . . . Their speech [is] a dialect of the Tartars . . ." (1865:96). They were also tall and "handsome timber'd people, out-wisted, pale and lean Tartarian visag'd," with black eyes, and smooth, curled, long, black hair; they were rarely bearded. They were readily recognized because of their flat noses (1865:96–97). Yet even this thorough-going endorsement was mitigated by the "Chronological Observations of America" attached to the book. There, under the date 3740 Anno Mundi, he stated "Hanno the *Carthaginian* flourished, who sent to discover the great Island *Atlantis,* i.e. *America.*"

Cotton Mather also gave the Tatarian theory a partial endorsement, though he was sure the British (Welsh) beat the Spanish to the New World (1820:I, 42–44). Writing around 1700 in his *Magnalia Christi Americana,* Mather told of a Russian who had traveled in Siberia and who reported that:

the inhabitants [of a certain island] go frequently upon the side of the *Frozen Sea* to hunt this monster [walrus?]; and because it requires great labor . . . carry their families . . . many times surprised with a sudden thaw, they are carried away . . . upon huge pieces of ice. . . . I am persuaded that several of those hunters have been carried upon those floating pieces of ice to the northern parts of America, which is not far from that part of Asia (1820:I, 42–44).

The fact "that the Americans who inhabit that country, which advances farthest toward the sea, have the same Physiognomy as those Islanders" confirmed his theory.

Not all Englishmen accepted the Anian route. Matthew Hale, in *The Primitive Origination of Mankind* (London, 1677), concluded that various people settled America at various times. Even though one could not determine for certain who had come to the New World first, Hale thought that either the British, Tatars, Chinese, or Carthaginians had gone there first (1677:195–197). The animals, however, gave him the same problems Acosta had faced ninety years earlier. Hale postulated "Necks of Land" which probably once connected the Old and New worlds. The animals probably came by land, but the sea route remained the most likely route for human migrations into America (1677:190–195; 202–203).

In the seventeenth century the English, and briefly the Dutch, carried the burden of the argument over Indian origins. This English interest probably reflected the greater number of Englishmen in the New World and the close religious, economic, and political contacts between the British and Dutch. It may have reflected besides greater freedom of publication in those two countries.

By the first quarter of the eighteenth century the Acostan Tradition had established itself more firmly in northern Europe than in Spain itself. The North produced no García or Barcia to argue that all possible theories were equally probable. It was not that the Acostan Tradition dominated the argument at any given moment, yet the tradition was consistently present. This tradition gained strength after 1728 when rumors of Russian expeditions under Bering began to reach Western Europe (Golder, 1922).

Before making a conclusion about the state of the debate over Indian origins, it is necessary to study one additional controversy which had a decided effect on the development of the discussion.

Toward New Criteria: La Peyrère and the "Pre-Adamites"

Sir Thomas Browne, in his popular *Religio Medici* of the 1640's, confessed "there are in Scripture stories that doe exceed the fables of Poets, and . . . my selfe could shew a catalogue of doubts, never yet imagined nor . . . resolved at first hearing" (1964:I, 31). Nevertheless, he continued,

. . . tis ridiculous to put off, or drowne the generall Flood of Noah in that particular inundation of Deucalion: that there was a Deluge once, seemes not to mee so great a miracle, as that there is not one alwayes. . . . There is another secret, not contained in the Scripture, which is more hard to comprehend, and put the honest Father to a Miracle; and that is, not only how the distinct pieces of the world, and divided Ilands should be first planted by men, but inhabited by Tygers, Panthers and Bears. How *America* abounded with beasts of prey, and noxious animals, yet contained not in it that necessary creature, a Horse. By what passage those, not only Birds, but dangerous and unwelcome Beasts came over: How there bee creatures there, which are not found in this triple continent; all which must needs bee stranger unto us, that hold but one Arke, and that the creatures began their progresse from the mountain of Ararat. Those who, to solve this, would make the Deluge particular, proceed upon a principle that I can in no way grant (1964:I, 31–33).

This suspicion of those who could explain how "that great Antiquity America lay buried for Thousands of years" (Browne, 1964:I, 135) by postulating a particular rather than a general Flood was closely connected to the outright rejection of those who derived any men from a source other than Noah, and through him, Adam. Paracelsus supposedly suggested the possibility that God might have made a second Adam for the New World, and many writers of the seventeenth and eighteenth century believed this attribution, though the book in which it supposedly appeared was lost (Bendyshe, 1865–1867:I, 353–355; Wright, 1928:211; García, 1729:248).

The concept of a particular Flood which nonetheless destroyed all the inhabited world found wide acceptance in the latter half of the seventeenth century (Allen, 1949:66–91; Woodward, 1702). The two-Adam theory, on the other hand, possessed few followers. Despite that, the best argument for the particular nature of the Deluge appeared anonymously with—and subordinate to—the best statement of the dual Adam thesis. In 1655 a book titled *Prae-Adamitae* was published at Amsterdam. The author, in the same year, published *Systema Theologicum ex Praeadamitarum Hypothesi. Pars Prima.*

These books ·shocked and delighted Europe and were immediate successes. Three new editions of the *Prae-Adamitae,* two of the *Systema,* and at least one edition containing both appeared before the end of the year. An English translation of *Prae-Adamitae, Men Before Adam,* and a second English volume containing both books came off the presses in 1656. A Dutch translation of the *Prae-Adamitae* appeared in 1661.

Despite the fact that both volumes were published anonymously, the author's name was no secret. Isaac de la Peyrère was a French Huguenot of some distinction even before he published the *Prae-Adamitae.* His *Traité du Rappel des Juifs* (1643) and his history of Greenland (1647) were well known. But these books had revealed no great interest in the problem of human origins. Barcia (García, 1729: "Proemio"), referring to La Peyrère's history of Iceland written in the 1640's and published in 1663, claimed that "La Peyrère affirmed it to be a vain and useless curiosity to investigate the Origin of the peoples."

The furious reaction to the *Prae-Adamitae* resulted in La Peyrère's forced conversion to Catholicism, a retraction (which, when published, went through at least four editions by 1663 and kept the affair alive), and the burning of the original book in Paris (McKee, 1944:456–459).

The manuscript of the *Prae-Adamitae* was written in the early 1640's. In 1643 La Peyrère showed it to a friend, and sometime within the next year he sent a copy to Hugo Grotius (McKee, 1944:456–457; La Peyrère, 1655:278). This book in conjunction with the *Systema* expounded the idea that biblical and historical evidence showed that men probably existed before Adam (La Peyrère, 1655; 1656; McKee, 1944; Maas, 1913; Philalethes, 1864; Winchell, 1880:454–461). The evidence lay in the puzzling statements in Romans 5:12–14 which indicated the existence of sin before Adam, the two creation stories in Genesis 1 and 2, and several other apparent contradictions. La Peyrère thought he could solve these puzzles by postulating that God made two creations: the first creation produced the gentiles who then spread over the world—even to America (La Peyrère, 1655:276–281); the second creation resulted in Adam, the progenitor of the Jews. The Deluge destroyed only the Hebrews. This theory explained why Egypt and Mesopotamia seemed more ancient than Israel, and why men seemed to be in America before the Flood.

The literary response to the *Prae-Adamitae* far surpassed the response to the Grotius-De Laet controversy. The subject of the pre-Adamites became for several years the favorite question with regard to human—and, largely incidentally, Indian—origins. In the year 1656 alone, in addition to La Peyrère's own works, at least twelve refutations were published. At least seven additional refutations appeared before 1698. Fabricius, in a doctoral dissertation of 1721, which purported to prove all men of "one and the same species," listed without dates thirty-seven more works touching on the subject of polygenism (Allen, 1949:133–137; Fabricius, 1865–1867:I, 372–377).

Most of the argument over polygenism centered on theology. When it touched on the origins of the Indians, it did so largely incidentally; but there was a close connection between the two controversies. Manasseh ben Israel (Roth, 1945:161–162) wrote a *Refutatio libri cui titulis Praeadamitae* which remained unpublished. He also corresponded with La Peyrère on occasion. Manasseh's gentile friend Paul Felgenhaur published *Der Prüfung über das lateinische Buch prae-Adamitae* (Amsterdam, 1659), which Fabricius considered so heretical that neither Lutherans nor the Dutch Reformed Church could claim its author (1865–1867:I, 377). Spitzel, the man who "buried" the Lost Tribes theory of Indian origins, wrote a criticism of polygenism in his *Infelix literatus* (Augsburg, 1680). Finally, Allen (1949:136 n. 103) says Joannes Pythius' *Responso exetastica* (1656) attempted to undermine La Peyrère's evidence by showing that the Americans got to the New World recently and by land.

Matthew Hale wrote his *Primitive Origination of Mankind* (1677) largely as a response to the polygenist turmoil. Despite the fact that "man is an Object of greatest vicinity to himself," men were likely "to remain ignorant of many things of importance concerning our selves" (1677:20). But he could not accept La Peyrère's polygenism because it undermined Scripture. Nor did he approve of the idea of a particular Flood, thus pre-Deluge men did not live in America. To get men to America Hale relied on ships; but the animals forced him to postulate "Necks of Land" connecting the Old and New worlds (1677:184–203).

The polygenist controversy spread even to Mexico. Sometime after 1729 Benito Jerónimo Feijóo Montenegro wrote his *Teatro crítico universal* and included in the *Teatro* a discourse called "Solución del gran problema histórico sobre la populación de la América, y Revoluciones del Orbe Terraques." Feijóo denounced polygenism and La Peyrère, who "vomitó tan pernicioso error," and made a rather vague endorsement of the Atlantean origin theory (1945:40–48).

Few Europeans openly supported polygenism; its theological implications forbade wide acceptance but the polygenist controversy did serve to advance the possibilities for determining American origins in a very fundamental way. Acosta first popularized the doubts about cultural comparisons, and drew attention to the geographical and faunal factors in a discussion of origins. Since 1589, men of the Acostan Tradition in both Spain and northern Europe had expanded on these doubts and factors. The general opinion of this school in 1729 was that the first men in America must have come from Tatary. The particular tribal source was beyond agreement, but the ancient Tatars (sometimes fused with the Scythians) were most frequently accepted.

Parallel to this growing acceptance of Tatary as the source of the Indian, there developed a rather dichotomous and confused attitude toward the Indians' culture. The Bible taught, by implication at least, diffusion of cultures. The Acostan Tradition implied a large degree of cultural independence, and some Acostans, like Samuel Purchas, explicitly endorsed the autocthonous creation of Indian cultures. But the primitive Indian cultures were not the major issue here; the high civilizations of Peru and Mexico had to be explained. Neither European theology nor the Renaissance experience of borrowing high culture from the ancients gave much theoretical support to autocthony. Consequently, Acostans had to resort to the Atlantic route to bring in the higher cultural characteristics. This presumed necessity to maintain a diffusionist position with respect to Peru and Mexico stymied development.

Adherence to the diffusionist position kept alive the belief that cultures—especially the more refined civilizations—could not be separated from a peoples' biological background; furthermore, it kept alive the assumption that cultural relationships implied physical relationships. Even though the Acostans brought in the Europeans only to account for Mexico and Peru (and sometimes the ruins of Central America), this very practice illustrates why the Garcían Tradition, with its emphasis on cultural comparisons and the general probability of all theories, could retain such vitality.

Until new criteria for determining the relationships between peoples could be developed, the comparative technique must be retained. Cobo (1653), Ogilby (1671), Josselyn (1674), and several others had used physiological comparisons in their theorizing, but none had thought out the extent to which this technique might prove useful.

The polygenists, by pointing up the possibility of genuinely different races—of men *not* descended from an ancestor common to all men—focused attention on the problem of race, of physique. The implications of polygenism went beyond the physical. Men who did not share ancestors need not share cultures. But this point should not be taken too strongly. Descendants of the gentile "Adam" would perhaps all show common cultural traits; the same held true for descendants of the Jewish Adam. But the gentiles had been around longer than the Jews (in the La Peyrère version of polygeny, not in all), or at least their antiquity was undeterminable; and no one could point to a "gentile" culture.

Though the gentiles might have differentiated, the same was less possible for the Jews. Consequently, Jewish relationships with other peoples could be traced through cultural similarities. But would the presence of a similarity indicate biological descent, or merely cultural contact? Gentile Christians borrowed heavily from Jews, but they were not of Jewish origin.

If culture were inconstant, physique was less so. The polygenist controversy served to draw attention to physique, thus increasing the possibility of creating new criteria for determining the source of a people through physical comparisons. Bendyshe (1865–1867:I, 360–364) reprinted an anonymous essay of 1684 which did attempt a classification of all men into races on the basis of physical characteristics. Around the same period comparative anatomy was becoming established; one of the early landmarks in that field, Tyson's *Ourang-Outang*, appeared in 1699. And Linnaeus' work reached the public in the 1720's. Archaeology too was achieving great popularity, especially in England, at the beginning of the eighteenth century (Daniels, 1963: 13–37).

A century would pass, however, before the archaeologist could develop the techniques to produce the material for the comparative anatomist to prove the ancient Americans were of this or that derivation. By then the question of the biological origin of the Indian had been relegated to a position of minor importance: the question had become largely a matter of cultural origins.

One should not expect the situation with respect to American Indian origins to be clearer in 1729 than before. Indeed, the opposite was true. What Europe had once viewed as a simple problem to be solved by a few simple associations of traits had become after two hundred years of study a very complex problem. No longer could one think only in terms of finding a single source for the Indian, his ordinary culture, and his great civilizations. The clarification of the subject via a separation of the various questions insured that no matter how strong the evidence indicating an unknown Siberian tribe as the progenitors of the American Indians, writers of the latter-day Garcían Tradition could bring their favorites across the Atlantic, or from under the Atlantic, with impunity.

General Conclusions

T HE ATTEMPTS of writers in the period of 1492 to 1729 to solve the questions relating to the origins of the American Indians are generally looked upon with an attitude ranging from contempt to indifference. Both extremes in attitude, in this writer's opinion, result from a misunderstanding of not only the intellectual conditions under which these early theorists wrote but also of their conclusions. The literature of the Middle Ages, wrote Bancroft (1886:I, 2–5), "consisted for the most part of musty manuscripts emanating from musty minds, utterly devoid of thought and destitute of reason." With this background, the early theorists of Indian origins did "not offer a theory as a suggestion of what might possibly be, but as a demonstration founded upon an unassailable basis."

Had Bancroft read more carefully García's discussion of the utility of *Opinión* from which he quoted (1886:I, 7–12), he would have recognized that much of the confusion of the early years was traceable to the fact that those "musty minds" were painfully aware that their bases were assailable. Justin Winsor (1889:I, 369), frequently referred to as the best authority on the history of the origin theories, said of the literature of the early period that "it is not characterized by much reserve in connecting races by historical analogies." The literature will not support such á conclusion, except in individual cases. It reveals a remarkable restraint not merely in connecting Indians with other peoples, but even in making any conclusion at all regarding a definite origin.

José Imbelloni's *La segunda esfinge indiana* (Buenos Aires, 1956) contains the best recent survey of the literature. Yet Imbelloni devoted so little attention to the pre-nineteenth century period that he thought García himself responsible for the 1729 edition of his book (Imbelloni, 1956:429). Then too, Imbelloni attributed a belief in a Jewish origin to several men who did not hold it (1956:25–26). Robert Wauchope, in common with many others, assumed that the earliest writers assigned the Indians to the Lost Tribes of Israel (1963:3). Yet that idea found its earliest expression around 1570.

Sometimes this lack of firsthand knowledge of the early writers is confounded by acceptance of distorted interpretations made by those who hold an exclusive view. Hyamson (1903:658) accepted Barbara Simon, a disciple of Lord Kingsborough's fanatical Jewish-Indian views, as an authority on early Spanish writers. As a result he divided the early theorists into two camps: those who held the Indians to be Jews; and those who thought the similarities between Indians and Jews to be the work of the devil. The first group included "Las Casas, Sahagún, Boturini, García, Gumilla (1740's), Beneventa [Motolinea], and Peter Martyr." The second included "Torquemada, Herrera, López de Gómara, Acosta" et al. Mrs. Simon found more supporters than her opinion really had, and credited her opponents with views they did not hold.

The greatest cause and object of confusion over the period before 1729 is the *Origen de los indios.* Those who write on the subject of Indian origins before 1729 all too often get their material from García and Barcia. Failure to understand that the *Origen* intended to substantiate *all* theories invalidates any use made of that book. A casual look at García can yield some surprising results. Winsor (1889:I, 369) thought García considered all theories "only to reject them all, and to favor a coming of Tartars and Chinese."

The best recent example of a misunderstanding of García comes from Don Cameron Allen's otherwise excellent *Legend of Noah*:

The most searching work on the origin of the Indians to appear in the first half of the seventeenth century was the *Origen de los indios de el nuevo mundo* of Gregorio García. García's book is a grand summary of all the theories that had been proposed prior to his time plus a critical examination of the tenability of each hypothesis. He completely overthrows the notion that the Indians arrived by sea and logically opposes the idea that the ancient world knew America under the name of Ophir or Tharsis. He rejects the theory that the Indians are Carthaginians, for he can find no similarities between the languages and customs of the Indians and those Punic peoples. The belief that the Indians are Jews has more value in it, because Indians and Jews are somewhat alike in customs, characters, language, and traditions; but he will not adhere to this notion. In similar wise, he presents the arguments of those who think that the Indians are descended from Romans, Greeks, Phoenicians, Chinese, Egyptians, Africans, Ethiopians, French, Cambrians, Kurlanders, Frisians, or Scyths. He favors the opinion of those who contend that the Indians are of Chinese or Scythian origin, but he will not stake his head on it. He suspects that the migration began shortly after the Flood and continued until recent times. The Indians, he believes, did not come from one nation but from many, and they arrived in the Americas by a variety of roads (1949:121–122).

Not only did the author of the above summation fail to notice the brackets signalizing Barcia's additions, but he also misunderstood García's "Parecer":

The Indians proceed neither from one Nation or peoples, nor went to those parts from only one [part] of the Old World, nor did the first Settlers walk or sail by the same road or voyage nor in the same time, nor in the same manner. But actually they proceeded from various Nations, from which some came by Sea, forced and driven by Storms, others by Art of Navigation looking for those Lands, of which they had heard. Some came by land. . . . Some came from Carthage . . . some from the Ten Tribes . . . Ophir . . . Atlantis . . . Greeks . . . Phoenicians . . . Chinese . . . Tartars . . . and other Nations (García, 1729:315).

Confusion over García's position is easily understood, because his intent is so readily missed, and because most writers use the 1729 edition without comprehending Barcia's contributions. But less understandably, immediately following the summation of García, Allen

(1949:122) writes: "Most of the historians writing in the early parts of the seventeenth century were so overwhelmed by the multiplicity of theories about the plantation of America that they were ready, like Acosta, to cut the Gordian knot by accepting all of them."

The casual student of Indian origins is little better off today than three hundred years ago. True, the consensus today is that the first Indians came to America by way of Siberia, but few archaeologists would care to identify the first people to come over, other than geographically. But, this belief that the Indians came from northeast Asia (geographically at least, and possibly biologically) is the *one* theme running throughout the writing of the seventeenth century. Other themes were current; but the Acostan Tradition was the one consistently held, elaborated, and refined.

The modern professional frowns upon trans-Atlantic contacts. Yet if the entire literature of the past twenty-five years were surveyed, it is possible the professional would be in a minority. Newspapers carry frequent stories about Old World cultural contacts with the Indians. The Austin *American-Statesman* (August 8, 1965) carried a New York *Times* report of an expedition to Mexico to trace an ancient dye used by Mexicans and Jews. The Dallas *Morning News* (January 18, 1966) printed a UPI story of a rabbi who thought King Solomon's ships came to America.

Theosophists and other cultists use Atlantean America in their occult theories (De Camp, 1954; Wauchope, 1962). This writer knows several college students—including some undergraduate anthropology majors—who insist on finding Greek artistic influences in Mayan culture. And shall the professional deny the amateur his Atlantic contacts when some of his own number hold to their theories of trans-Pacific migrations (Ekholm, 1964)?

How is the modern layman to treat such men as Harold Gladwin? His work in Southwestern archaeology is of high repute, but his *Men Out of Asia* (1947) is a curious mixture of archaic and modern thinking. Yet the volume is not treated badly by Magowan and Hester in their popular *Early Man in the New World* (1962). The Gladwin book is a good example of a man trapped by his ideology to as great an extent as any man of the sixteenth or seventeenth century was trapped by his theology. Gladwin does not believe that the same invention—industrial processes, complex social formulae—could have been made by two different peoples; hence, if an invention exists ten thousand miles from where he thinks it originated, he is certain someone took it there. On the other hand, the followers of the late Arthur Posnansky think that all civilization originated in America. Furthermore, the Lost Tribes still wander around the New World—the Mormons hold the Jewish descent of the Indians as an article of faith (Wauchope, 1962:50–68).

The greatest single advantage our own age has over the first two centuries of the origin debate is that we now have a recognizable professional discipline which treats of such things. The interested layman can discover these professionals, who have their differences, but generally agree on major points. Professionals write the accepted texts, and they train new generations of professionals and laymen in terms of the current consensus.

In *form* this does not appear greatly different from the propagation of the sixteenth- and seventeenth-century theological consensus by professional theologians. But anthropology as a professional discipline has more recently achieved its status. Before that, there were no professional experts whose study would include the problems concerning man in the New World.

A thorough study of the literature on the origins of the American Indians before 1729 reveals that the theorists of that age reached the limits of the accepted methodology near the beginning of the seventeenth century. It reveals also that they continued their theorizing in ways sometimes ludicrous, but generally serious. The tradition I have labeled "Garcían" was characteristically credulous, but nonetheless aware of the limits of "proof." The Acostan Tradition was characteristically restrained, and far more aware of the need for new techniques in investigating relationships between peoples.

Both these traditions used the methods available to them as efficiently as any modern practitioner. If they failed to solve the question of Indian origins, the fault lay not so much in themselves as in the failure of their descendants to provide them with the information and techniques necessary to a solution.

BIBLIOGRAPHY

Acosta, Joseph de

1590 *Historia natural y moral de las Indias.* Sevilla: En Casa de Juan de León.

1940 *Historia natural y moral de las Indias.* Edmundo O'Gorman (ed.). 1st ed., México: Fondo de Cultura Económica.

1962 *Historia natural y moral de las Indias.* Edmundo O'Gorman (ed.). 2d ed., México: Fondo de Cultura Económica.

1963 *The Natural and Moral History of the Indies.* Edward Grimston (trans.). C. R. Markham (ed.). Reprint ed., 2 vols. New York: Burt Franklin.

Albinus, Peter

1884 *A Treatise on Foreign Languages and Unknown Islands.* Edmund Goldsmid (trans. and ed.). Edinburgh: Unwin Bros. of London, printer.

Allen, Don Cameron

1949 *The Legend of Noah. Renaissance Rationalism in Art, Science, and Letters.* "Illinois Studies in Language and Literature," Vol. XXXIII, Nos. 3 and 4. Urbana: University of Illinois.

Amann, E.

1935 "Preadamites," *Dictionnaire de Théologie Catholique,* Vol. XII, Pt. 2, Cols. 2793–2800.

Anglería, Pedro Mártir de

1944 *Décadas del Nuevo Mundo.* Joaquín Torres Asensio (trans.). Buenos Aires: Editorial Bajal. First published between 1511 and 1530.

Anonymous

1865– "A New Division of the Earth, According to the Different Spe-
1867 cies or Races of Men who Inhabit it," *Memoirs read before the Anthropological Society of London 1863–1864.* 3 vols. London: The Society. I, 360–364.

Apocrypha
   1957   *The Apocrypha of the Old Testament. Revised Standard Version.* New York: Nelson.
Arber, Edward (ed.)
   1885   *The First Three English Books on America.* Birmingham: Printed by Turnbull and Spears of Edinburgh.
Arias Montano, Benito
   1572   "Phaleg, sive de gentium sedibus primis, orbisque terrae situ," in the *Biblia Sacra* ("Polyglot Bible of Antwerp"). Antwerp, 1569–1572.
Arriaga, Pablo Joseph de
   1920   *La extirpación de la idolatría en el Perú.* Horacio H. Urteaga and Carlos A. Romero (eds.). "Colección de libros y documentos referentes a la historia del Perú," 2d ser. Vol. 1. Lima: Sanmartí. First published Lima, 1621.
Atkinson, Geoffroy
   1929   *La Littérature géographique française de la renaissance. Répertoire Bibliographique.* Paris: Editions Auguste Picard.
Ávila, Francisco de
   1942   *De Priscorum Huaruchiriensium Origine et Institutis.* Hippolyte Galante (ed.). Madrid: Instituto Gonzalo Fernández de Oviedo. First published in Lima, 1608, as "Tratado y relación de los errores, falsos dioses y otras supersticiones . . . de las provincias de Huarochiri."
Babcock, William H.
   1922   *Legendary Islands of the Atlantic. A Study in Medieval Geography.* New York: American Geographical Society.
Baldwin, John D.
   1872   *Ancient America, in Notes on American Archaeology.* New York: Harper & Brothers.
Bancroft, Hubert Howe
   1886   "On the Origins of the Americans," *The Native Races of the Pacific States.* 5 vols. V, 1–132. San Francisco: The History Company.
Barcia Carballido y Zúñiga, Andrés González de
   1729   See García, 1729
Barlow, Roger
   1932   *A Brief Summe of Geographie.* E. G. R. Taylor (ed.). London: Hakluyt Society, Ser. 2, Vol. 69. Written 1540–1541.

Bell, Aubrey F. G.
  1922   *Benito Arias Montano.* Oxford: Oxford University Press, "Hispanic Notes and Monographs," No. 5.

Benavides, Alonso de
  1945   *Fray Alonso de Benavides' Revised Memorial of 1634.* Cyprian J. Lynch (ed.). Peter P. Forrestal (trans.). Albuquerque: University of New Mexico Press.

Bendyshe, T.
  1865–   "The History of Anthropology," *Memoirs read before the An-*
  1867   *thropological Society of London 1863–1864.* 3 vols. London: The Society, I, 335–458.

Bennett, John W.
  1966   "Comments on 'The Renaissance Foundations of Anthropology'," *American Anthropologist,* 68 (1966), 215–220.   See Rowe, 1965, 1966.

Benzoni, Giralmo
  1857   *History of the New World, by Giralmo Benzoni, Milan, Shewing His Travels in America, From A.D. 1541 to 1556: with some particulars of the Island of Canary.* W. H. Smyth (trans.). London: The Hakluyt Society, Ser. 1, Vol. 21. First published Venice, 1565.

Betanzos, Juan Diaz de
  1880   *Suma y narración de los Incas.* Marcos Jiménez de la Espada (ed.). Madrid: M. G. Hernández.

Biographie Universelle
  1854–   *Biographie Universelle Ancienne et Moderne.* 2d ed. Paris:
  1865   Madame C. Desplaces.

Botero, Giovanni
  1599   *Relaciones universales del mundo de Iuan Botero Benes, Primera y Segunda parte.* Diego de Aguiar (trans.). Valladolid: por los herederos de Diego Fernández de Córdova. First published Rome, 1591, as *L'relatione universali.*

Bourne, William
  1578   *Booke Called a Treasure for Travellers.* London: Thomas Woodcocke.
  1963   *A Regiment for the Sea and other Writings on Navigation.* E. G. R. Taylor (ed.). Cambridge: The Hakluyt Society.

Bouyssonie, A. and J.
  1935 "Polygénisme," *Dictionnaire de Théologie Catholique.* Vol.
        XII (Paris, 1935), Pt. 2, Cols. 2520–2536.
Brerewood, Edward
  1614 *Enquiries Touching the Diversity of Languages and Religions
        Through the Chief Parts of the World.* London: J. Bill.
Browne, Thomas
  1964 *The Works of Sir Thomas Browne.* Geoffrey Keynes (ed.).
        4 vols. Chicago: University of Chicago Press. "Religio Med-
        ici." First published 1636. "Hydriotaphia, Urne-Buriall."
        First published 1658.
Cabello Valboa, Miguel de
  1945 *Obras.* Jacinto Jijón y Caamaño (ed.). Vol. I, Quito: Edito-
        rial Ecuatoriana. MS of the "Miscelánea Anthártica," completed
        by 1586.
  1951 *Miscelánea Anthártica, una historia del Perú antiquo.* Luis E.
        Valcárcel (ed.). Lima: Universidad Nacional de San Marcos,
        Facultad de Letras, Instituto de Etnología.
Calancha, Antonio de la
  1638 *Corónica moralizada del orden de San Augustín en el Perú con
        sucesos egenplares en esta monarquía.* Barcelona: Pedro Laca-
        vallería.
  1939 *Crónica moralizada (Páginas selectas).* Gustavo Adolfo Otero
        (ed.). La Paz: Artística.
Cárdenas, Juan de
  1913 *Primera parte de los problemas y secretos maravillosos de las
        Indias.* 2d ed. Mexico: Museo Nacional de Arqueología, His-
        toria y Etnología. First published Mexico, 1591.
Casas, Bartolomé de las
  1909 *Apologética historia sumaria cuanto a las cualidades, disposición,
        descripción, cielo y suelo de estas tierras, y condiciones naturales,
        policías, repúblicas, maneras de vivir y costumbres de las gentes
        de estas Indias occidentales y meridionales, cuyo imperio soberano
        pertenece a los Reyes de Castilla.* M. Serrano y Sanz (ed.).
        Madrid: Bailly Bailliere e hijos. Written by 1550.
  1951 *Historia de las Indias.* Agustín Millares Carlo (ed.). México:
        Fondo de Cultura Económica. Written by 1559.
  1957– *Historia de las Indias.* Juan Pérez de Tudela and Emilio López
  1961 Oto (eds.). 2 vols. Madrid: Real Academia Española.

1958   *Apologética historia* . . . Juan Pérez de Tudela Bueso (ed.).
        Madrid: Real Academia Española.
1966   *Los indios de México y Nueva España. Antología.* Edmundo
        O'Gorman (ed.). México: Porrúa.

Castellanos, Juan de
1955   *Elegías de varones ilustres de Indias.* 4 vols. Bogotá: Editorial
        A B C. First published 1589 ("Part I" only).

Castillo Tejero, Neomi, and Lorena F. Mirambell Silva
1962   *Bibliografía antropológica. Trabajos publicados en México
        1955–1962.* México: 35th Congress of Americanists.

Cervantes de Salazar, Francisco
1914   *Crónica de la Nueva España.* M. Magallón (ed.). Madrid:
        Hispanic Society of America. Completed ca. 1570.

Cieza de León, Pedro
1554   *Parte Primera de la Chrónica del Perú.* Anvers: Iuan Steelsio.
        First edition, Sevilla, 1553.
1941   *Primera parte de la cronica del Perú.* Madrid: Espasa–Calpe.

Clarke, Hyde
1886   "Examination of the Legend of Atlantis in reference to Proto-
        historic Communication with America," *Transactions of the Royal
        Historical Society*, N.S. III (1886), 1–46.

Cobo, Bernabé
1890–   *Historia del Nuevo Mundo.* Marcos Jiménez de la Espada
1893   (ed.). 4 vols. Sevilla: E. Rasco. Completed by 1653.

Colón, Cristobal
1960a   *The Journal of Christopher Columbus.* Cecil Jane (trans.).
        L. A. Vigneras (ed.). New York: Albert and Charles Boni.
1960b   "The Letter of Christopher Columbus describing the results of
        his first voyage," in Colón, 1960a:191–202.

Colón, Fernando
1892   *Historia del Almirante Don Cristóbal Colón.* Madrid: T. Minu-
        esa. Completed 1539, published 1571.
1947   *Historia del Almirante Don Cristóbal Colón.* México: Fondo de
        Cultura Económica.

Comtaeus, Roberti (Robert Comte)
1644   *De Origine Americanarum Dissertatio.* Nicolaus Herouart
        (ed.). Amsterdam: Nicolai Ravesteinii.

Córdova Salinas, Diego de
1958   *Crónica Franciscana de las Provincias del Perú.* Lino G. Canedo (ed.). New ed. Washington, D.C.: Academy of American Franciscan History. First published Lima, 1651.

Costa, Cándido
1900   *As duas americas.* 2d ed. Lisboa: Jose Bustos.

Cubero Sebastián, Pedro
1682   *Peregrinación del mundo.* Nápoles: Carlos Porsil.
1684   *Descripción general del mundo y notables sucessos dél.* Nápoles: Salvador Castaldo. This was designed to be "Part II" of the *Peregrinación.*

Curzola, Vicente Palatino de
1943   "Tratado del derecho y justicia de la guerra que tienen los reyes de España contra las naciones de la India occidental," in Lewis U. Hanke, 1943: 11–37.

Daniel, Glyn
1963   *The Idea of Prehistory.* Cleveland & New York: World Publishing Co.

Dávila Padilla, Agustín
1625   *Historia de la fundación y discurso de la Provincia de Santiago de México, de la Orden de Predicadores.* Brussels. First published Madrid, 1596.
1955   *Historia de la fundación . . .* Agustín Millares Carlo (ed.). México: Academia Literaria.

De Camp, L. Sprague
1954   *Lost Continents. The Atlantis Theme in History, Science, and Literature.* New York: Gnome Press.

Dictionnaire de Théologie Catholique contenant l'exposé des doctrines de la
1908–   *théologie Catholique, leurs preuves et leur historie . . .*   15 vols.
1935   Paris: Letouzey et Aní, 1908–1935.

Durán, Diego
1951   *Historia de las Indias de Nueva España y Islas de Tierra Firme.* José F. Ramírez and Alfredo Chavero (eds.). 3 vols. México: Editoria Nacional. Written by 1580.

Dury, John
1650   "An Epistolicall Discourse of Mr. Iohn Dury to Mr. Thorowgood. Concerning his conjecture that the Americans are descended from the Israelites. With the History of a Portugall Iew,

Antonie Monterinos, attested by Manasseh Ben Israel, to the same effect," in Thorowgood, 1650, paged independently.

Eden, Richard (trans.)

1885 *The Decades of the Newe Worlde or West India.* Pedro Mártir de Anglería, in Arber, 1885. Original translation, 1555.

Ekholm, Gordon

1964 "Transpacific Contacts," in Jesse D. Jennings and Edward Norbeck (eds.). *Prehistoric Man in the New World.* Chicago: The University of Chicago Press, for William M. Rice University.

Eliot, John

1660 "The Learned Conjectures of Reverend Mr. John Eliot touching the Americans, of New and notable consideration, written to Mr. Thorowgood," in Thorowgood, 1660:1–28.

D'Engel, E. Bailli (Samuel)

1767 *Essai sur cette question: Quand et comment l'Amerique a-t-elle été peuplée d'hommes et d'animaux?* 5 vols. Amsterdam: M. M. Rey.

Esdras IV, R. H. Charles (ed.). *The Apocrypha and Pseudepigrapha of the Old Testament.* 2 vols. Oxford: Clarendon Press, 1913.

Estete, Miguel de

1924 *Noticia del Perú.* Lima: Sanmartí. "Coleccion de libros y documentos referentes a la historia del Perú," 2d ser. Vol. 8, pp. 1–71.

L'Estrange, Hamon

1652 *Americans no Iewes, or Improbabilities that the Americans are of that Race.* London: by W. W. for Henry Seile.

Eyries

1854–1865 "Horn (George)," *Biographie Universelle,* XIX, 640–641.

1854–1865 "Laet (Jean de)," *Biographie Universelle,* XXII, 439–440.

Fabricius, Jo. Alberto

1865– "Dissertatio Critica de hominibus orbis nostri incolis, specie et
1867 ortu avita inter se non differentibus. . . ." English translation by T. Bendyshe in *Memoirs read before the Anthropological Society of London 1863–1864.* ·3 vols. London:. The Society, 1865–1867. I, 372–420. First published 1721.

Federmán, Nicolás

1958 *Historia indiana.* Juan Friede (ed. and trans.). Madrid: Artes Gráficas. First published 1557.

Feijóo y Montenegro, Benito Jerónimo
   1945   "Solución del gran problema histórico sobre la populación de la
          América, y Revoluciones del Orbe Terraques," in *Dos Discursos
          de Feijóo sobre América.*   México: Biblioteca Enciclopedia popu-
          lar.   Written and published in the 1730's.
Felgenhaur, Paul
   1659   *Der Prüfung über das lateinische Buch prae-Adamitae.*   Amster-
          dam.
Fernández, Diego
   1876   *Primera y segunda parte de la historia del Perú.*   Manuel Odrio-
          zola (ed.).   Lima: "Colección de documentos literarios del
          Perú."   Vols. 8–9.   First published 1571.
Fernández de Enciso, Martín
   1530   *Suma de geographia q̃ trata de todas las partidas y provincias del
          mundo: en especial de las Indias.*   2d ed.   Sevilla: J. Crom-
          berger.   First published 1519.
   1897   *Descripción de las Indias occidentales.*   José T. Medina (ed.).
          Santiago de Chile: Imprenta elzeviriana.
Fernández de Piedrahita, Lucas
   1688   *Historia general de las conquistas del Nuevo Reyno de Granada*
          [Amberes: J. B. Verdussen].
   1942   *Historia general de las conquistas del Nuevo Reino de Granada.*
          4 vols.   Bogotá: Editorial A B C.
Galvão, Antonio
   1862   *The Discoveries of the world, from their first Original Unto the
          Year of Our Lord, 1555.*   Admiral Bethune (ed. and trans.).
          London: The Hakluyt Society, Ser. 1, Vol. 30.   First published
          in Portuguese, 1555.
García, Gregorio
   1729   *Origen de los indios de el nuevo mundo, e Indias occidentales*
          . . .   Andrés González de Barcia Carballido y Zúñiga (ed.).
          Madrid: Francisco Martínez Abad.   First published 1607.
Garcilaso de la Vega, el Inca
   1945   *Primera parte de los commentarios reales, que tratan del origen
          de los Yncas* . . .   Ángel Rosenblat (ed.).   2 vols.   Buenos
          Aires: Emecé.   First published 1609.
Garreyre, J.
   1935   "La Peyrère (Isaac de)," *Dictionnaire de Théologie Catholique,*
          Vol. VIII, Pt. 2, Cols. 2615–2616.

Genebrard, Gilbert

  1567 *Chronographia in duos libros distincta. Prior est de rebus veteris populii (G. G. auctore); posterior, recentes historias . . . coplectitur (A. Pontaco . . . auctore).* 2 pts., Paris.

Gladwin, Harold

  1947 *Men Out of Asia.* New York: McGraw-Hill.

Godbey, Allen Howard

  1930 *The Lost Tribes a Myth—Suggestions Towards Rewriting Hebrew History.* Durham [N.C.]: Duke University Press.

Golder, F. A.

  1922 *Bering's Voyages. An Account of the Efforts of the Russians to Determine the Relation of Asia and America.* 2 vols. New York: American Geographical Society.

Greenlee, William Brooks (trans. and ed.)

  1938 *The Voyages of Pedro Alvares Cabral to Brazil and India From Contemporary Documents and Narratives.* London: The Hakluyt Society, Ser. 2, Vol. 81.

Grotius, Hugo

  1642 *De Origine Gentium Americanarum. Dissertatio.* Paris. Also in De Laet, 1643.

  1643 *De Origine Gentium Americanarum. Dissertatio Altera adversus obtrectatorem, opaca quem bonum facit barba.* Paris. Also in De Laet, 1644.

  1884 *On the Origin of the Native Races of America. A Dissertation.* Edmund Goldsmid (trans.). Edinburgh: Unwin Bros. of London, printers. See also Henry W. Haynes, 1888.

Hakluyt, Richard

  1903 *The Principal Navigations, Voyages, Traffiques, & Discoveries of the English Nation . . .* 12 vols. Glasgow: J. MacLehose and Sons. First published 1589.

Hale, Matthew

  1677 *The Primitive Origination of Mankind, considered and examined According to the Light of Nature.* London: Wm. Godbid for Wm. Shrowsbery.

Hanke, Lewis U.

  1935 *The First Social Experiments in America. A Study of the Development of Spanish-Indian Policy in the Sixteenth Century.* Cambridge: Harvard University Press.

1937   "Pope Paul II and the American Indians," *The Harvard Theo-logical Review,* XXX (April, 1937), 65–102.

1943   *Cuerpo de documentos del siglo XVI sobre los derechos de España en las Indias y las Filipinas.* Lewis Hanke (ed.). México: Fondo de Cultura Económica.

1952   *Bartolomé de Las Casas, Historian. An Essay in Spanish Histori-ography.* Gainesville: University of Florida Press.

1959   *Aristotle and the American Indians. A Study in Race Prejudice in the Modern World.* Chicago: Henry Regnery.

1965   *The Spanish Struggle for Justice in the Conquest of America.* Boston: Little Brown and Company. First published 1949.

Hanke, Lewis U. and Manuel Giménez Fernández (eds.)

1954   *Bartolomé de las Casas 1474–1566. Bibliografía crítica y cuerpo de materiales para el estudio de su vida, escritos, actuación y polé-mica que suscritaron durante cuatro siglos.* Santiago de Chile: Fondo Histórico y Bibliográfico José Toribio Medina.

Harrisse, Henry

1958   *Bibliotheca Americana Vetustissima. A Description of the Works Relating to America published between the Years 1492 and 1551.* Madrid: Librería General V. Suárez. See also Sanz, 1960.

Haynes, Henry W.

1888   "Goldsmid's Translation of Grotius' 'On the Origins of the Na-tive Races of America'," *The Nation,* XLVI (March 15, 1888), 216. See Grotius, 1884.

Herrera y Tordesillas, Antonio de

1934– *Historia general de los hechos de los castellanos en las Islas y*
1957   *Tierra Firme del Mar Océano.* Antonio Ballesteros-Baretta (ed.). 17 vols. Madrid: Atlas.

1944– *Historia general . . .* J. Natalicio González (ed.). 10 vols.
1947   Asunción de Paraguay and Buenos Aires: Editorial Guaraní. First published 1601–1613.

Hodgen, Margaret

1964   *Early Anthropology in the Sixteenth and Seventeenth Centuries.* Philadelphia: University of Pennsylvania Press.

Horn, Georg

1669   *De Originibus Americanis Libri Quatuor.* Hemipoli: Joannis Mudliri. First published 1652.

Hornberger, Theodore
1939 "Acosta's *Historia natural y moral de las Indias*. A Guide to the Source and the Growth of the American Scientific Tradition," *Texas Studies in English*, No. 19 (1939), pp. 139–162.

Hyamson, Albert M.
1903 "The Lost Tribes, and the Influence of the Search for them on the Return of the Jews to England," *Jewish Quarterly Review*, XV (1903), 640–676.

Imbelloni, J.
1956 *La segunda esfinge indiana*. Buenos Aires: Librería Editorial Hachette. First published 1927.

Isagoge
1935 *Isagoge histórica apologética de las Indias Occidentales y especial de la Provincia de San Vicente de Chiapa y Guatemala . . .* J. Fernando Juárez Muñoz (ed.). Guatemala: Tipografía Nacional. First published 1892 from MS. of ca. 1711.

Ixtlilxóchitl, Fernando de Alva
1952 *Obras históricas*. Alfredo Chavero and J. Ignacio Dávila Garibi (eds.). 2 vols. México: Editoria Nacional. Materials date from 1608–1616.

Jennings, Jesse D., and Edward Norbeck (eds.)
1964 *Prehistoric Man in the New World*. Chicago: The University of Chicago Press for William M. Rice University.

Josselyn, John
1865 *An Account of Two Voyages to New-England Made during the years 1638, 1663 . . .* Boston: W. Veazie. First published 1674.

Laet, Joannes de
1640 *L'Histoire de Nouveau Monde ou Description des Indies Occidentales . . .* Leyden: Elseviers. First published 1625.
1643 *Notae ad Dissertationem Hugonis Grotii "De Origine Gentium Americanarum," et Observationes aliquot ad meliorem indaginem difficillimae illus Quaestionis*. Amsterdam: Ludovicum Elzevirium.
1644 *Responsio ad Dissertationem Secundum Hugonis Grotii, De Gentium Americanarum, cum Indice ad utrumque libellum*. Amsterdam: Ludovicum Elsevirium.

Landa, Diego de

 1941 *Relación de las cosas de Yucatán.* Alfred M. Tozzer (ed. and trans.). Cambridge [Mass.]: Peabody Museum.
 1959 *Relación* . . . Ángel M. Garibay (ed.). México: Porrúa.

León Pinelo, Antonio

 1943 *El Paraíso en el Nuevo Mundo. Comentario apologético, Historia Natural y Peregrina de las Indias Occidentales Islas de Tierra Firme del Mar Océano* . . . Raúl Porras Barrenechea (ed.). 2 vols. Lima: Comité del IV Centenario del Descubrimiento del Amazonas. Written ca. 1650–1656.

Lery, Jean de

 1957 *Histoire d'un voyage fait en la terre du Bresil, autrement dite Amerique.* Paris: Editions de Paris. First published 1578.

Lescarbot, Marc

 1907 *The History of New France* . . . 3 vols. Toronto: Champlain Society *Publications,* Vols. 1 (1907), 7 (1911), and 11 (1914). First published 1609.

Lizana, Bernardo de

 1892 *Historia y conquista espiritual de Yucatán.* México: Museo Nacional. Written by 1633.

Lizárraga, Reginaldo de

 1946 *Descripción de las Indias. Crónica sobre el Antiguo Perú, concebida y escrita entre los años 1560 a 1602* . . . Francisco A. Loayza (ed.). Lima. Completed 1602, first published 1907.

López Cogolludo, Diego

 1688 *Historia de Yucathan.* Francisco de Ayeta (ed.). Madrid: Juan García Infanzón. Written by 1659.

López de Gómara, Francisco

 1941 *Historia general de las Indias.* 2 vols. Madrid: Espasa-Calpe. First published 1552.

Lumnius, Joannes Fredericus

 1569 *De Extremo Dei Iudicio et Indorum vocatione.* Venice: Apud Dominicum de Farris. First published 1567.

McKee, David R.

 1944 "Isaac de la Peyrère, a precursor of Eighteenth-Century Critical Deists," *Publications of the Modern Languages Association,* LIX (1944), 456–485.

Maas, A. J.
 1913 "Preadamites," *The Catholic Encyclopedia,* XII (New York: The Encyclopedia Press, 1913), 370–371.

Magalhães, Pero de
 1922 *The Histories of Brasil.* John B. Stetson (trans.). 2 vols. New York: The Cortés Society. Written in the 1570's.

Magowan, Kenneth, and Joseph A. Hester, Jr.
 1962 *Early Man in the New World.* New York: Doubleday for The American Museum of Natural History.

Manasseh ben Israel
 1652 *The Hope of Israel.* Moses Wall (trans.). London: Livewell Chapman. Third printing of trans. made in 1650.
 1881 *Origen de los americanos. Esto es esperanza de Israel.* Santiago Pérez Junquera (ed.). Madrid: S. Pérez Junquera. First published 1650.

Mariana, Juan de
 1780– *Historia general de España.* 15th impression. 2 vols. Ma-
 1782 drid: Andrés Ramírez. First published 1592.

Martín, Enrico
 1606 *Reportorio de los tiempos, y historia natural desta Nueva España.* México: Emprenta del mesmo autor.
 1948 *Reportorio de los tiempos é historia natural de Nueva España.* México: Secretaria de Educación Pública.

Mather, Cotton
 1820 *Magnalia Christi Americana: or, the Ecclesiastical History of New-England from its first planting in the Year 1620, Unto the Year of Our Lord 1698.* 2 vols. Hartford: Silas Andrus, Roberts & Burr, printers. First published 1702.

Matienzo, Juan
 1910 *Govierno del Perú.* Buenos Aires: Compañía sud-americana de billetes de banco. Written ca. 1566–1573.

Means, Philip A.
 1923 "Some Comments on the Inedited Manuscript of Poma de Ayala," *American Anthropologist,* N.S.; XXV (1923), 397–405.

Medina, Balthassar de
 1682 *Chrónica de la Santa Provincia de San Diego de México, de religiosos descalços de N.S.P.S. Francisco en Nueva-España.* México: Juan de Ribera.

Medina, Jose Toribio
1898– *Biblioteca Hispano-Americana (1493–1810)*. 7 vols. Santiago
1907 de Chile: En casa del autor.

Mendieta, Gerónimo de
1870 *Historia eclesiástica indiana*. Joaquín García Icazbalceta (ed.).
México: Antigua-Librería. Written ca. 1596.

Meulen, Jacob Ter, and P. J. J. Diermanse (eds.)
1950 *Bibliographie des escrits imprimes de Hugo Grotius*. The
Hague: Martinus Nijhoff.

Montesinos, Fernando de
1882 *Memorias antiguas historiales y políticas del Perú*. Marcos Jiménez de la Espada (ed.). Madrid: Imprenta de M. Ginesta.
Written by 1644.
1920 *Memorias antiguas* . . . P. A. Means (trans.). London: The
Hakluyt Society, Ser. 2, Vol. 48.
1930 *Memorias antiguas* . . . Lima: Sanmartí. "Colección de libros
y documentos referentes a la historia del Perú," Ser. 2, Vol. 6.

Morton, Thomas
1947 *New English Canaan; or New Canaan, Containing An Abstract in
Three Bookes*. New York: Peter Smith. First published 1637.

Morúa, Martín de
1922– *Origen de los reyes del gran Reino del Perú*. 2 vols. Lima:
1925 Sanmartí. "Colección de libros y documentos referentes a la
historia del Perú," Ser. 2, Vols. 4 and 5. Written 1590, first
published 1911.

Motolinía, Toribio [de Benevente, or]
1941 *Historia de los indios de la Nueva España*. Daniel Sanchez
(ed.). México: Chávez Hayhoe. Written ca. 1541.

Nodal, Bartholomé García de, and Gonzalo de
1753 *Relación del viage, que por orden de su magestad, y acuerdo de el
Real Consejo de Indias hicieron . . . al descubrimiento del Estrecho nuevo de San Vicente . . . y reconocimiento del de Magallanes
. . . 1621*. 2d impression. Cádiz: M. Espinosa de los Mon-
teros [1753].

Ocampo, Florián de
1553 *Los cinco primeros libros de la Corónica general de España . . .*
Alcalá [1553]. First edition 1544. 1553 edition expanded.

Ogilby, John
   1671   *America: Being the Latest, and Most Accurate Description of the New World* . . . London: John Ogilby.
O'Gorman, Edmundo
   1951   *La idea del descubrimiento de América. Historia de esa interpretación y crítica de sus fundamentos.* México: Centro de Estudios Filosóficos.
Oliva, Anello
   1895   *Libro primero del manuscrito original del R. P. Anello Oliva, S. J. Historia del Reino y Provincias del Perú.* Lima: San Pedro.
Ovalle, Alonso de
   1646   *Histórica relación del Reyno de Chile, y de las missiones, y ministerios que exercita en el la Compañia de Iesus.* Rome: Francisco Cavallo.
Oviedo y Valdés, Gonzalo Fernández de
   1851–   *Historia general y natural de las indias islas y Tierra-Firme del*
   1855   *Mar Océano.* 4 vols. Madrid. First published 1535–1550. Incomplete.
   1944–   *Historia general* . . . Jose Amador de los Ríos (ed.). Asun-
   1945   ción de Paraguay: Editorial Guaranía.
   1950   *Sumario de la natural historia de las Indias.* José Miranda (ed.). México: Fondo de Cultura Económica. First published 1526.
Pennington, Loren E.
   1966   *Hakluytus Posthumus: Samuel Purchas and the Promotion of English Overseas Expansion.* Emporia, Kansas: "The Emporia State Research Studies," Vol. XIV (March, 1966), No. 3.
Pérez de Ribas, Andrés
   1645   *Historia de los triumphos de nuestra santa fee entre gentes las más bárbaras, y fieras del nuevo Orbe* . . . Madrid: Alõso de Paredes.
Peyrère, Isaac de la
   1655   *A Theological Systeme upon that Presupposition That Men were before Adam.* London. Published first in Latin in 1655. This translation actually appeared in 1656 bound with La Peyrère, 1656.
   1656   *Men before Adam. Or a Discourse upon the twelfth, thirteenth, and fourteenth Verses of the Fifth Chapter of the Epistle of the Apostle Paul to the Romans. By which are prov'd that the first Men were created before Adam.* London. First published 1655.

Philalethes

1864 "Peyrerius and Theological Criticism," *The Anthropological Review*, II (1864), 109–116.

Poissons, Jean Baptiste

1644 *Animadversiones ad ea quae Hugo Grotius et Johannes Labetius de Origine Gentium Peruvianarum et Mexicanarum scripserunt.* Paris.

Polo de Ondegardo, Juan

1916– *Informaciones acerca de la religión y gobierno de los Incas.* 2
1917 vols. Lima: Sanmartí. "Colección de libros y documentos referentes a la Historia del Perú," Vols. 3 and 4. Written ca. 1571.

Poma de Ayala, Phelipe Guamán

1936 *El Primer nueva corónica y buen gobierno.* Paul Rivet (ed.). Paris: Institut d'ethnologie. Facsimile of MS. Written ca. 1587–1615.

1944 *La Obra de Phelipe Guamán Poma de Ayala "Primer nueva corónica y buen gobierno."* Arthur Posnansky (ed.). La Paz: Instituto "Tihuanacu" de antropología.

1956 *La nueva crónica y buen gobierno.* Luis Bustos Galvesz (interpreter). Vol. I. Lima: Editorial Cultura.

Posnansky, Arthur

1945 *Tihuanacu. The Cradle of American Man.* James F. Shearer (ed. and trans.). 2 vols. in 1. New York: J. J. Augustín. Has parallel Spanish and English texts.

Prince, Carlos

1915 *Origen de los indios de América. Origen y civilizaciones de los indígenas del Perú.* Lima: En casa del autor.

Purchas, Samuel

1613 *Purchas his Pilgrimage, or Relations of the World and the Religions observed in all ages and places discovered, from the Creation unto this Present.* London: Wm. Stansby for Henrie Fetherstone.

1617 *Purchas his Pilgrimage . . .* 3d ed. enlarged. London: Wm. Stansby for Henrie Fetherstone.

1905– *Hakluytus Posthumus, or Purchas His Pilgrimes Contayning a*
1906 *History of the World in Sea Voyages and Lande Travells by Englishmen and others.* 20 vols. Glasgow: J. MacLehose and Sons. First published 1625.

Pythius, Joannes
  1656 *Responso exetastica ad tractatum, incerto Authore, nuper editum, cui titulis: Praeadamitae.* Lugduni Batavi.

Raleigh, Walter
  1820 *The History of the World in Five Books.* New ed. 6 vols. Edinburgh: Archibald Constable & Co.

Rastell, John
  1848 *The Interlude of the Four Elements: An Early Moral Play.* J. O. Holliwell (ed.). In *Early English Poetry, Ballads, and Popular Literature of the Middle Ages.* Vol. XXII. London: The Percy Society. Published ca. 1520 as "A new Interlude and a mery, of the nature of the iiij Elements, declarynge many proper poyntes of Phylosophy Naturall, and Divers Straunge Landys, and of Dyvers Straunge Effectes and Causis."

René-Moreno, Gabriel
  1905 "Fray Antonio de la Calancha," in *Bolivia y Perú. Notas históricas y bibliográficas.* 2d ed., pp. 1–84. Santiago de Chile: Imprenta Litografía y Encuadernación Barcelona.

Rivet, Paul
  1960 *As origens do homem americano.* Paulo Duarte (trans.). 3d ed. Saõ Paulo: Anhambi, 1960. First published 1943.

Rocha, Diego Andrés
  1891 *Tratado único y singular del origen de los indios del Perú, Méjico, Santa Fé y Chile.* Madrid: J. C. García. "Colección de libros raros o curiosos que tratan de América." Vols. 3 and 4. First published 1681.

Rochefort, Charles
  1666 *The History of the Caribby Islands.* John Davies (trans.). London: by J. M. for T. Dring and J. Starkey. First published 1658.

Román y Zamora, Jerónimo
  1897 *Repúblicas de Indias idolatrías y gobierno en México y Perú antes de la conquista.* 2 vols. Madrid: J. García. "Colección de libros raros o curiosos que tratan de América." Vols. 14 and 15. First published 1575.

Roth, Cecil
  1937 *Magna Bibliotheca Anglo-Judáica. A Bibliographical Guide to Anglo-Jewish History.* New ed. London: Jewish History Society.

1938   *Anglo-Jewish Letters (1158–1917)*. London: The Soncino Press.
1945   *A Life of Menasseh ben Israel. Rabbi, Printer, and Diplomat.* [2d ed.?], Philadelphia: Jewish Publication Society of America. First published 1934.

Rowe, John H.
1965   "The Renaissance Foundations of Anthropology," *American Anthropologist*, Vol. 67 (1965), pp. 1–20.
1966   "Further Notes on the Renaissance and Anthropology: A Reply to Bennett," *American Anthropologist*, Vol. 68 (1966), pp. 220–222.

Sabin, Joseph
1962   *Bibliotheca Americana. A Dictionary of Books relating to America from its Discovery to the Present Time.* Reprint ed. 29 vols. in 15. Amsterdam: Israel.

Sahagún, Bernardino de
1956   *Historia general de las cosas de Nueva España.* Angel M. Garibay (ed.). 4 vols. México: Porrúa.

Sancho, Pedro
1917   *An Account of the Conquest of Peru.* P. A. Means (ed. and trans.). New York: The Cortés Society. Written in 1534.

Santa Cruz Pachacuti Yamqui, Juan de
1873   "An account of the Antiquities of Peru," in Clements R. Markham (ed.) *Narratives of the Rites and Laws of the Yncas.* London: The Hakluyt Society, Ser. 1, Vol. 48, pp. 67–122.
1927   "Relación de antigüedades deste reyno del Perú." Lima: Sanmartí. "Colección de libros y documentos referentes a la historia del Perú." 2d ser., Vol. 9, pp. 125–235. Written in 1613.

Santisteban Ochoa, Julián
1946   *Los cronistas del Perú.* Cusco: D. Miranda.

Sanz, Carlos
1960   *Bibliotheca Americana Vetustissima. Ultimas adiciones.* 2 vols. Madrid: Librería General V. Suárez. See also Harrisse, 1958.

Sarmiento de Gamboa, Pedro
1952   *Historia de los Incas.* Ángel Rosenblat (ed.). Buenos Aires: Emecé. Written ca. 1572, first published in 1906.

Schmidel, Ulrich
  1891 *A True and agreeable description of some principal Indian lands and islands* . . . Lui L. Domínguez (trans.). London: The Hakluyt Society, Ser. 1, Vol. 8. First published 1567.

Schubert, Herta
  1962 *Arias Montano y el Duque de Alba en los Países Bajos.* Santiago de Chile & Madrid: Cruz del Sur.

Sewall, Samuel
  1886– *Letter-Book of Samuel Sewall.* Boston: Historical Society.
  1888 "Collections," 6th Ser. Vols. 1 and 2.

Sharrow, Bernard
  1947 "British Colonial Conceptions of American Indian Origins." Unpublished Master's thesis, Columbia University.

Simon, Barbara
  1836 *The Ten Tribes of Israel Historically Identified with the Aborigines of the Western Hemisphere.* London: R. B. Seeley and W. Burnside.

Simón, Pedro
  1627 *Primera parte de las noticias historiales de las conquistas de Tierra Firme en las Indias Occidentales.* Cuenca: Domingo de la Iglesia.
  1882– *Noticias historiales* . . . Medardo Rivas (ed.). 5 vols.
  1892 Bogotá: M. Rivas.

Smith, John
  1808– "The General History of Virginia, New England, and the Sum-
  1814 mer Isles," in John Pinkerton (ed.) *A General Collection of the Best and Most Interesting Voyages and Travels in all parts of the World.* 17 vols. London: Longman, Hurst, Rees, and Orme.

Solórzano y Pereyra, Juan de
  1629– *Disputationem de indiarum iure* . . . Madrid: F. Martinez.
  1639
  1703 *Política indiana.* Amberes: J. Verdussen. First Spanish version, 1648.
  1930 *Política indiana.* 5 vols. Madrid and Buenos Aires: Compañía ibero-americano. Based on the Francisco Ramírez de Valenzuela edition of 1736–1739.

Spitzel, Gottlieb
 1661   *Elevatio relationis Montezinianae de repertis in America tribus Israeliticis . . .* Basle.
Staden, Hans
 1874   *The Captivity of Hans Stade of Hesse, in A.D. 1547–1555 among the Wild Tribes of Eastern Brazil.* Albert Tostal (trans.). Richard Burton (ed.). London: The Hakluyt Society, Ser. 1, Vol. 51.
Strachey, William
 1953   *The History of Travell into Virginia Britania.* R. H. Major (ed.). London: The Hakluyt Society, Ser. 2, Vol. 103. Written 1612.
Suárez de Peralta, Juan
 1878   *Tratado del descubrimiento de las Indias y su conquista . . .* Justo Zaragoza (ed.). Madrid. Written ca. 1580.
 1949   *Noticias históricas de Nueva España.* Justo Zaragoza (ed.). México: Secretaría de Educación Pública. Reprint of 1878 edition.
Taylor, E. G. R.
 1930   *Tudor Geography, 1485–1583.* London: Methuen.
 1934   *Late Tudor and Early Stuart Geography, 1583–1650. A Sequel to Tudor Geography, 1485–1583.* London: Methuen.
Thevet, André
 1944   *Singularidades da Franca Antarctica a que outros chaman da America.* Estevão Pinto (trans.). São Paulo: Bibliotheca Pedagógica Brasileiro. First published 1557, in French.
Thorowgood, Thomas
 1650   *Iewes in America, or, Probabilities that the Americans are of that Race. With the removal of some contrary reasonings, and earnest desires for effectual endeavours to make them Christian.* London: by W. H. for Tho. Slater.
 1660   *Jews in America, or, Probabilities that those Indians are Judaical made more probable by some Additionals to the former conjectures.* London: for Henry Brome.
Torquemada, Juan de
 1723   *Primera (Segunda, Tercera) Parte de los veinte i un libros rituales i monarchia indiana, con el origen y guerras de los Indios Occidentales . . .* Andrés Barcia (ed.). 3 vols. Madrid: N. Rodríguez Franco. First published 1613.

Tovar, Juan de

1944 *Relación del origen de los indios que habitan esta Nueva España según sus historias.* Manuel Orozca y Berra (ed.). México: Editorial Leyenda.

Vanegas de Bustos, Alejo

1898 *Primera Parte de las differencias de libros q̃ ay en el universo.* First published 1540. Selections on America reprinted in Medina, 1898–1907:I, 162–165.

Vargas Machuca, Bernardo de

1892 *Milicía y descripción de las Indias.* 2 vols. Madrid: V. Suárez, "Colección de libros raros o curiosos que tratan de América," Vols. 8 and 9. First published 1599.

1913 *Apologías y discursos de las conquistas occidentales.* París and Buenos Aires.

Vázquez de Espinosa, Antonio

1942 *Compendium and description of the West Indies.* Charles Upson Clark (trans.). Washington, D.C.: Smithsonian Misc. Coll., Vol. 102. Part on America published 1630.

1948 *Compendio y descripción de las Indias Occidentales.* Charles Upson Clark (ed.). Washington, D.C.: Smithsonian Misc. Coll., Vol. 108.

Vespucci, Amérigo

1951 *El Nuevo Mundo. Cartas relativas a sus viajes y descubrimientos.* Roberto Levillier (ed.). Buenos Aires: Editorial Nova. Materials date from 1500–1504.

Vetancurt, Augustín de

1698 *Teatro mexicano. Descripción breve de los sucessos exemplares, históricos, políticos, militares, y religiosos del nuevo mundo occidental de las Indias.* México: Doña María de Benavides Viuda de Juan de Ribera.

Villagomes, Pedro de

1919 *Exortaciones e instrucción acerca de las idolatrías de los indios del Arzobispado de Lima.* Lima, 1649: Sanmartí. "Colección de libros y documentos referentes a la historia del Perú." Vol. 12.

Villagutierre Sotomayor, Juan de

1701 *Historia de la conquista de la provincia de Itza.* Madrid: Lucas Antonio de Bedmar, y Narváez.

Wagner, Godofredus
  1669 *De Originibus Americanis. Dissertationem . . .* Leipzig.
Wauchope, Robert
  1962 *Lost Tribes and Sunken Continents. Myth and Method in the Study of American Indians.* Chicago: The University of Chicago Press.
Williams, Arnold
  1948 *The Common Expositor. An Account of the Commentaries on Genesis, 1527–1633.* Chapel Hill: The University of North Carolina Press.
Wilmsen, Edwin N.
  1965 "An Outline of Early Man Studies in the United States," *American Antiquity,* XXXI (Oct., 1965), 172–192.
Winchell, Alexander
  1890 *Preadamites, or a demonstration of the Existence of Men Before Adam; Together with a Study of Their Condition, Antiquity, Racial Affinities, and Progressive Dispersion over the Earth.* 5th ed., Chicago: S. C. Griggs.
Winsor, Justin
  1889 "The Progress of Opinion Respecting the Origin and Antiquity of Man in America," in *Narrative and Critical History of America.* 8 vols. Boston and New York: Houghton, Mifflin and Co.
Wolf, Lucien (ed.)
  1901 *Menasseh ben Israel's Mission to Oliver Cromwell. Being a Reprint of the Pamphlets published by Menasseh ben Israel to promote the "Re-admission of the Jews to England" 1649–1656.* London: Macmillan Company.
Woodward, John
  1702 *An Essay towards a Natural History of the Earth, and Terrestrial Bodies, especially Minerals . . .* 2d ed. London. First published 1700.
Wright, Herbert
  1928 "The Controversy of Hugo Grotius with Johan de Laet on the Origin of the American Aborigines," in Herbert Wright (ed.) *Some Less Known Works by Hugo Grotius,* pp. 211–228. First published *Catholic Historical Review,* III (1917), 257–275.

Xérez, Francisco de

1891 *Verdadera relación de la conquista del Perú y provincia del Cuzco llamada la Nueva Castilla* ... Madrid: J. García.

Zamora, Alonso de

1945 *Historia de la provincia de San Antonio del Nuevo Reino de Granada.* 4 vols. Bogotá: Biblioteca Popular de Cultura Colombina. First published 1701.

Zárate, Agustín de

n.d. *Historia del descubrimiento y conquista de la provincia del Perú,* in Julio de Riverend (ed.) *Crónicas de la conquista del Perú.* México: Editorial Nueva España. First published 1555.

Zimdars, Benjamin Frank

1965 "A Study in Seventeenth-Century Peruvian Historiography: The Monastic Chronicles of Antonio de la Calancha, Diego de Córdova Salinas, and the *Compendio y Descripción* of Antonio Vázquez de Espinosa." Austin [Texas]: Unpublished Ph.D. dissertation, The University of Texas.

INDEX

Acosta, Joseph de: background of, 48–
49; implications of arguments of, 53–
54; influence on Herrera, 58; translation of work, 78; use by northern
Europeans of, 114–121 *passim*
Acostan tradition: defined, 13, 60; in
seventeenth-century Spain, 101–106;
elaboration of in northern Europe,
78, 125–128, 137–138; modern anthropology and, 147
Adam: as progenitor of Indians, 9, 31;
and New World Adam, 9–10. *See also*
Paracelsus; Peyrère, Isaac de la; polygenism
African origin theory: 107. *See also*
Ethiopian origin theory
Allen, Don Cameron: on Spitzel, 135;
on García, 145–146; on Acosta, 146–
147
America: relation to Asia, 4, 5, 6, 9;
pre-Columbian discovery of, 18, 21,
25, 81–82, 135. *See also* land bridge
Anglería, Pedro Martir de: on Ophir,
4, 7; on Hebrews in America, 33
Anian, Straits of: location of, 59; connection with America of, 69, 125. *See
also* land bridge; Scythian origin theory; Tatar origin theory
animals in America: origins of, 4, 5, 8,
9, 10, 50, 52, 66–67, 97, 113–114;
migration to America, 66–67, 80, 97,
101, 104–105, 113–114, 137; unique
species of, 67–68. *See also* land bridge
antediluvian man in America. *See* Indians, antiquity of
Antipodes: 11, 49
archaeology:: Las Casas and, 24; rise of,
53–54
architecture, Indian: European influence
on, 28–29, 66, 81

Arias Montano, Benito: on Ophirian
origin theory, 41–42; mentioned, 72,
112, 124
Arias Mountanus. *See* Arias Montano,
Benito
Aristotle: on Burning Zone, 11; on
Carthaginian discovery of "America,"
17
Ark, of Noah: and search for Indian
origins, 9, 10, 95; landing place of,
9, 95, 96; second Ark of, 49
Arsareth: in America, 35, 37, 39; mentioned, 51, 69
Arzareth. *See* Arsareth
Asia: and America, 4, 5, 6, 9. *See also*
land bridge; Scythian origin theory;
Tatar origin theory
Atlantean origin theory: accepted, 25,
28, 30, 141; rejected, 51, 56, 80;
García on, 72; in northern Europe,
112
Atlantis: settlement of, 30; sinking of,
30; location of, 30, 92; Josselyn on,
136; mentioned, 23, 65, 90
authority: methodological, 12, 55–56
autocthony: cultural, 29, 51, 52–53, 116,
117, 126–127; biological, 46, 51,
141–143; methodology and, 126–127;
polygenism and, 141–143. *See also*
polygenism
Aztec migration myths: influence of, 37,
39, 40

Babel: 43
Balboa: on Negroes in Panama, 8
Barcia, Andrés. *See* Barcia Carballido y
Zúñiga, Andrés González de
Barcia Carballido y Zúñiga, Andrés Gon-
zález de: and García's *Origen,* 79,
106–107; on Horn, Georg, 125

Basques: Indians and, 90–92. *See also* Spanish origin theory (Basque)

beards. *See* hair

Benavides, Alonso de: on Chinese origin theory, 100

Benzoni, Giralmo: on Carthaginian origin theory, 28

biblical commentaries: use of, 11

biblical exegesis: as methodological tool, 40

Brerewood, Edward: on Tatar origin theory, 114–115; arguments of, 115

Browne, Sir Thomas: on Deluge, 138

Burning Zone: 11

Cabello Valboa, Miguel de: goals of, 42; and Ophirian origin theory, 42–43; and Carthaginian origin theory, 43; and Hebrew origin theories, 44. *See also* Cubero Sebastián, Pedro

Calancha, Antonio de la: on Hebrew origin theories, 85; on Spanish origin theories, 89; on antediluvian settlement of America, 95; critique of Pedro Simón, 98; basis of theories, 100; on Japhethite origin theory, 100; on Tatar origin theory, 100

Cambrian origin theory: 107

Canaan: as progenitor of Indians, 37–38; curse of, 98

Canaanite origin theory: discussion of, 37–38; and Hebrew origin theories, 38; in northern Europe, 113

Canary Islanders: and American Indians, 4; shipwrecked in America, 123

Cárdenas, Juan: 56

Carthaginian merchants: discovery of America by, 17, 65

Carthaginian origin theory: accepted, 16, 20–21, 26, 27, 28–29, 37, 56, 80, 81, 85, 92, 124–125; rejected, 20, 23, 28, 43, 56, 80, 81, 116; relation to Phoenician origin theory, 21, 108, 124–125; García on, 66–69; Josselyn on, 136; mentioned, 28, 56, 97, 112. *See also* Phoenician origin theory

Casas, Bartolomé de las: and Columbus' *Journal*, 4; on East Indian origin theory, 22; on Atlantis, 23; on antiquity of Indians, 23–24; Hebrew origin theories and, 23, 34; on López de Gómara, 25

Cervantes de Salazar, Francisco: on Atlantean origin theory, 28

Chinese origin theory: accepted, 27–28, 31, 100, 120–121; García on, 73–74; rejected, 122

Christ, death of: guilt of Indians in, 70–71, 88; discovery of America and, 96

Christianity in America, pre-Columbian: 30–31, 120

Christianization of Indians. *See* Indians, Christianization of

ciencia. See methodology, García's four ways to knowledge

circumcision: in Yucatán, 8, 23, 33, 51

Cobo, Bernabé: background, 102–103; use of physical characteristics, 103–105; use of Solórzano, 104

Colón, Cristobal. *See* Columbus, Christopher

Colón, Fernando: dispute with Oviedo, 19–20

Columbus, Christopher: in Ophir, 4; on New World, 4–5

Columbus, Ferdinand. *See* Colón, Fernando

Comtaeus, Roberti. *See* Comte, Robert

Comte, Robert: on Phoenician and Carthaginian origin theories, 124–125

conquistadores: as ethnographers, 16

Courlander origin theory: proposed, 59–60; mentioned, 100, 107

Cuba: visited by Hanno, 26; part of Atlantis, 30

Cubero Sebastián, Pedro: plagiarism, 83

Curzola, Vicente Palatino de: on Carthaginian origin theory, 28–29

customs: as indications of origins, 27–28, 30, 38, 39, 70–71, 97–98. *See also* methodology

Danish origin theory: 107
Dávila Padilla, Agustín: on Carthaginian origin theory, 56
De Laet, Joannes. *See* Laet, Joannes de
Deluge: date of, 12; universality of, 138–139
Durán, Diego: on Hebrew origin theory (Lost Tribes), 38
Dury, John: 129–130

East Indian Origin theory: accepted, 22, 44–45, 58–59. *See also* Scythian origin theory; Tatar origin theory
Eden. *See* Paradise
Eden, Richard: 27
Egyptian origin theory: 37, 85, 107
elephants in America: 95
Eliot, John: on Hebrew origin theories, 134
Esdras: source for story of Ten Lost Tribes of Israel, 35, 36–37, 39, 69, 87; criticized, 69–70, 84–85, 115, 120; mentioned, 34, 51
Española: site of Ophir, 4, 7, 23, 33; visited by Carthaginians, 18, 20, 26, 27; remnant of Atlantis, 30
Estotiland (Labrador): 58
L'Estrange, Hamon: on Brerewood, 133; reply to Thorowgood, 133
Ethiopian origin theory: accepted, 37, 120; García on, 107; rejected, 124
Ethiopians: in Panama, 8
experience: as methodological test, 11–12, 49

Fabricius: on polygenism, 140
Fé Divina. See methodology, García's four ways to knowledge
Fé Humana. See methodology, García's four ways to knowledge
Feijóo Montenegro, Benito Jerónimo: on Atlantean origin theory, 141; on La Peyrère, 141
Felgenhaur, Paul: 140
Fernández de Piedrahita, Lucas: on Japhethite origin theory, 84

French origin theory: 107
Frisian origin theory: 107

Galvão, Antonio: on Chinese origin theory, 27–28
García, Gregorio: background, 60; purpose of work, 60–61; methodology of, 61–64; conclusions of, 74; misinterpretations of, 145–146
Garcían Tradition: defined, 13, 76; elaborated, 74–76; strength of in 1729, 106–109, 143; modern writers and, 147–148
Genebrard, Gilbert: on Hebrew origin theories, 35; used by García, 69; mentioned, 72, 77, 111, 124
gentile: defined, 84
giants in America: 95
Gladwin, Harold: 147–148
Gómara, Francisco López de. *See* López de Gómara, Francisco
Greek origin theory: proposed, 30; García on, 73
Grimston, Edward: translator of Acosta's work, 78
Grotius, Hugo: background of, 118; on Ethiopian origin theory, 120; on Norse origin theory, 120; on Chinese origin theory, 120–121; mentioned, 78, 111

hair: climatic conditions and, 68–69, 94, 102; Cobo's observations on, 103–104; mentioned, 113
Hakluyt, Richard: on Welsh origin theory, 57; on Spanish authors, 111
Hale, Matthew: on first Americans, 137; on polygenism, 140–141
Ham, curse of. *See* Canaan, curse of
Hanno: in America, 26, 27, 43; mentioned, 65, 136
Hebrew origin theory (general): early comment on, 23, 29, 31; discussed, 33–35; attributed to Las Casas, 34. *See also* Hebrew origin theory (Issa-

char); Hebrew origin theory (Lost Tribes)

Hebrew origin theory (Issachar): proposed, 86; accepted, 86, 87; rejected, 86, 87; basis of, 98. *See also* Hebrew origin theory (general); Hebrew origin theory (Lost Tribes)

Hebrew origin theory (Lost Tribes): early development, 33, 34–40; accepted, 35–40, 85–86, 88, 93–94, 128–135 *passim*; rejected, 34, 44, 51, 84, 85, 120, 128–135 *passim*; considered, 69, 96, 113; García on, 69–71; in seventeenth century Spain, 84–88; "Hope of Israel" controversy, 128–135. *See also* Hebrew origin theory (general); Hebrew origin theory (Issachar)

Hebrews, Ten Lost Tribes of: identified as Tatars, 114; mentioned, 33

Herrera y Tordesillas, Antonio de: influenced by Acosta, 58

Hespérides, Islas: identified as West Indies, 18, 20

Hespéro (mythical king of Spain): 18

Horn, Georg: in Barcia, 107; background, 119; De Laet and, 124; mentioned, 111

Hosea: use of in Hebrew origin theories, 39

Iberians. *See* Basques
Iectan. *See* Joktan
Imbelloni, J.: 33, 145
Indians: early comments on, 3–4, 5, 6, 7; unity of accepted, 3–4, 98, 103–104; Christianization of, 8, 21–22, 29, 132; enslavement of, 15, 21–22, 24
———, antiquity of: 23–24, 61, 116, 121, 127, 135; antediluvian existence of, 37, 80, 95–96, 99, 140
———, character of: as humans, 14–15; as rational, 14–15, 21–22; mentioned, 3, 5, 24, 29–30

———, civilization of. *See* autocthony
Irish origin theory: 107
Israel, Ten Lost Tribes of. *See* Hebrews, Ten Lost Tribes of
Issachar. *See* Hebrew Origin Theory (Issachar)

Japheth: as progenitor of Indians, 32, 84, 100
Jewish origin theory. *See* Hebrew origin theories
Jews. *See* Hebrews
Joktan: father of Ophier, 42; connection with Yucatán, 42, 88
Josselyn, John: on Atlantis, 136; on Carthage, 136; on Tatars, 136

Kircher, Athanasius: on Egyptian origin, 107
Kirchmaier, George Kaspar: 125

Laet, Joannes de: on Acosta, 78; background of, 118–119; on Chinese origin theory, 122; on Norse origin theory, 122; on Tatar-Scythian origin theory, 122–123; on Canary Islanders, 123; on Ethiopian origin theory, 123; on Madoc, 123; on Polynesian origin theory, 123
Landa, Diego de: on Hebrew origin theory, 29
Land bridge, between Old and New World: Oviedo on, 18; Acosta on, 49, 50–51; significance of, 52, 99, 101–102; discussed in northern Europe, 121, 135, 137
languages of Indians: diversity of, 3–4, 66, 71, 88, 104; and Old World languages, 91–92, 97–98. *See also* word comparison
La Peyrère, Isaac de. *See* Peyrère, Isaac de la
Lapp origin theory: possibility of, 58, 100

Las Casas, Bartolomé de. *See* Casas, Bartolomé de las

León Pinelo, Antonio: on Paradise, 96

Lescarbot, Marc: on Atlantis, 112; on Spanish origin theories, 112; on Lost Tribes, 113; on Canaanite origin theory, 113

Lizárraga, Reginaldo de: on Carthaginian origin theory, 56

Ljung, Ericus: 125

López de Gómara, Francisco: on Indians, character of, 24; on America, pre-Columbian discovery of, 25; on Atlantis origin theory, 25

Lost Tribes. *See* Hebrews, Ten Lost Tribes of

Lumnius, Joannes Fredericus: proposes Hebrew origin theory, 34–35

Madoc: in America, 57, 117. *See also* Welsh origin theory

Magalhães, Pero de: on Chinese origin theory, 31

Magellan, Ferdinand: effect of voyage of, 5, 8, 9

Manasseh ben Israel: background of, 129; connection with Montesinos, Antonio, 129; gentile scholars and, 129; on Hebrew origin theory, 131; "Hope of Israel" controversy and, 130–133; on pre-Adamites, 140

Martín, Enrico: on Courlander origin theory, 59–60

Mather, Cotton: on Thorowgood, 134; on Welsh origin theory, 136, on Tatar origin theory, 136–137

Medea. See Seneca, *Medea*

Medina, Balthassar de: on Issachar, 88; on Joktan, 88

Mendieta, Gerónimo de: 57

methodology: discussion of, 10–13, 74–76, 97–109 *passim*, 125–128 *passim*, 138–143 *passim*; García's four ways to knowledge and, 62–64, 89, 96, 107–108; Thorowgood on, 134

monsters. *See* animals, unique species

Montesinos, Antonio de: background of, 128–129

Montesinos, Fernando de: on Ophirian origin theory, 82–83

Morton, Thomas: on Trojan origin theory, 112

navigation: use of by ancients, 9

New World: early concept of, 4–6

Noah: relation to Indians, 9, 30, 65

Norse origin theory: 58, 107, 120, 122

Ocampo, Florián de: on Hanno, 27

Ogilby, John: on Lost Tribes, 135; on Tatars and Scythians, 135, 136

Ophir (person): son of Jokton, 42; in Far East, 43; in America, 83

Ophir (place): location of, 4, 7, 23, 33, 42, 65; biblical references to, 41

Ophirian origin theory: discussion of, 36, 40, 41–42, 43, 82–84, 87; relation to other theories, 40–41, 100; García on, 72; relation to Solomon, 82; in northern Europe, 112–113, 124

opinión. See methodology, García's four ways to knowledge

Ovalle, Alonso de: 97

Oviedo y Valdéz, Gonzalo Fernández de: purpose of work, 16; on Carthaginian origin theory, 16–18; on Spanish origin theory (Basque), 18–19; refutation by Fernando Colón of, 19–20

Panama: Ethiopians in, 8

Paracelsus: idea of two Adams, 9–10, 138; polygenism, 12

Paradise: Old World location of, 9; in New World, 95–96

Paria: 7

Peleg: 42

Pérez de Ribas, Andrés: on Tatar origin theory, 101

Peru: derivation of name of, 42, 57, 79, 112

Peter Martyr. *See* Anglería, Pedro Martir de

Peyrère, Isaac de la: polygenism, 11, 12; background of, 139; pre-Adamites, 139–141. *See also* polygenism

Phaleg. *See* Peleg

Phoenician origin theory: discussion of, 81, 107, 112, 125; connection of with Carthaginian origin theory, 21, 73. *See also* Carthaginian origin theory

physical characteristics: as indicators of origin, 28, 31. *See also* hair; skin color

Poissons, Jean Baptiste: on Ophirian origin theory, 124

polygenism: attributed to Paracelsus, 9–10, 12, 138; Isaac de la Peyrère on, 11, 12, 139–141; relation of to Deluge, 138–139; pre-Adamite controversy, 139–141; Indian origins and, 141–143. *See also* Adam; Paracelsus; Peyrère, Isaac de la

Polynesian origin theory: possibility of, 123

Poma de Ayala, Phelipe Guamán: 45–46

Posnansky, Arthur: on autocthony, 46

Powell, David: on Welsh origin theory, 57

pre-Adamites. *See* polygenism

Purchas, Samuel: on Spanish authors, 11; on Carthaginians, 112; on Brerewood, 115–116; on autocthony, 116

Pythius, Joannes: on polygenism, 140

Rastell, John: 27, 110

Rocha, Diego Andrés: on Spanish origin theory (Basque), 90–93; on Hebrew origin theory (Lost Tribes), 93–94; on Tatars in America, 93–94; work compared to García's, 94

Rochefort, Charles: on Lost Tribes, 134–135

Román y Zamora, Jerónimo: on pre-Columbian Christianity in America, 30–31; on Indian origins, 31

Sahagún, Bernardino de: on Aztec folk history, 31–32; on Hebrew origin theory, 32

Sarmiento de Gamboa, Pedro: on Ulysses, 30; on Atlantean origin theory, 30–31

Scythian origin theory: García on, 73–74; use by Rocha of, 92–93, 94; mentioned, 107, 121, 136; relation of to Tatar origin theory, 121, 122–123

Scythians: early comparison with Indians, 7

Seneca, *Medea*: relevance to origins of Indians, 25–26, 65

Sewall, Samuel: on Thorowgood, 134

Shalmaneser: 35, 85

Shemite origin theory: 133

Simon, Mrs. Barbara Ann: on partisans of Hebrew origin theory, 33, 145

Simón, Pedro: on Issachar, 86, 87; on antediluvian Americans, 95; on animals of America, 97; Calancha on, 98; methodology of, 98

skin color: cause of, 7, 43, 94; as indicative of origin, 100, 103

Smith, John: on Carthaginian origin theory, 111–112

Solomon: 7, 72, 82

Solórzano y Pereyra, Juan de: on Issachar, 86–87; on Spanish origin theory (Gothic), 89; on Paradise, 95; on García, 96–97; on animals, 97; methodology of, 99; on Tatar origin theory, 101

Spain, claim to Indies of: 18, 29, 92–93

Spanish origin theory (Basque): proposed, 18–19; Fernando Colón on, 19; García on, 72; Rocha on, 90–93; mentioned, 31, 85

Spanish origin theory (Canarian). *See* Canary Islanders

Spanish origin theory (general): in

seventeenth-century Spain, 88–94; in North Europe, 112

Spanish origin theory (Gothic): rejected, 26, 73, 89

Spanish origin theory (Hesperian). *See* Spanish origin theory (Basque)

Spanish origin theory (Moorish): *See* Spanish origin theory (Gothic)

Spanish origin theory (Roman): 73, 81

Spitzel, Gottlieb: on Lost Tribes, 135; on polygenism, 140

Sporades: 65

Strachey, William: on Canaanite origin theory, 113

Suárez de Peralta, Juan: on Lost Tribes, 36–37; on other theories, 37–38

Tarshish: location of, 65

Tartars. *See* Tatars

Tatar origin theory: Chinese origin theory and, 73–74; support for, 100, 101, 102, 109, 114–115, 116, 122–123, 125–126, 136–137; Scythian origin theory and, 121, 122–123

Tatars: compared to Indians, 6; Lost Tribes and, 69, 71; Scythians and, 93–94

Ten Lost Tribes of Israel. *See* Hebrews, Ten Lost Tribes of

Thorowgood, Thomas: Dury and, 130; Lost Tribes and, 130, 131–132; methodology of, 134

Thule: location of, 25–26

Tihuanacu: autocthony and, 46

Torquemada, Juan de: Las Casas and, 34; on Hebrew origin theory, 34, 84–85; on animals, 97; on Tatar origin theory, 100

trans-Atlantic migration: belief in, 21,

105–106, 117, 127; discussed, 50–65, 109, 113–114

Trojan origin theory: 107, 112, 117

Ulysses: in Yucatán, 30

Vanegas de Bustos, Alejo: on Carthaginian origin theory, 21, 43, 66

Vázquez de Espinosa, Antonio: on Issachar, 86, 87, 88; on other theories, 87, 88

Vespucci, Amerigo: on New World, 5–6

Vetancurt, Agustín de: on antediluvian Americans, 95; methodology of, 96

Villagutierre Sotomayor, Juan de: 97

Vos, Isaac: 119

Wagner, Godofredus: 125

Wauchope, Robert: on Hebrew origin theory, 33, 145

Welsh origin theory: 57, 116, 136. *See also* Madoc

Winsor, Justin: on early theorists, 144

word comparison: validity of, 23, 30, 37, 44, 49, 91–92. *See also* languages of Indians

writing: Indian knowledge of, 8, 29, 44, 51, 66, 70–71, 122

Yucatán: Greeks in, 30; derivation of name of, 42, 88; Ethiopians in, 120

Zamora, Alonso de: on Hebrew origin theory, 84; on Japhethite origin theory, 84

Zárate, Agustín de: on Atlantean origin theory, 28

VERMONT COLLEGE
MONTPELIER, VERMONT